Making Sure of Maths
Book 1

T. F. Watson, M.A., F.E.I.S., and T. A. Quinn, M.A.

Published by Holmes McDougall Ltd, Edinburgh
Printed by Banks & Co. Edinburgh,
Designed by Bob Crawford

7157 0750—7

Contents

Up and down the number ladder

A Going up

Look at this ladder.
How many steps has it?
Start at step 3. Go up 2 more and we come to 5.
So 2 more than 3 is 5.

20 19 18 17 16 15 14 13 12 11 10 9 8 7 6 5 4 3 2 1

1 Use the ladder to find the number that is:

(**a**) 2 more than 6 (**b**) 2 more than 10
(**c**) 3 more than 4 (**d**) 4 more than 5
(**e**) 4 more than 10 (**f**) 5 more than 3
(**g**) 6 more than 4 (**h**) 6 more than 8
(**i**) 7 more than 3 (**j**) 8 more than 7
(**k**) 10 more than 5 (**l**) 7 more than 9

Going down

Start at step 9. Go down 4 and we come to step 5.
So 4 less than 9 is 5.

2 Use the ladder to find the number that is:

(**a**) 3 less than 8 (**b**) 3 less than 10
(**c**) 4 less than 9 (**d**) 5 less than 12
(**e**) 6 less than 14 (**f**) 7 less than 15
(**g**) 5 less than 15 (**h**) 5 less than 20
(**i**) 10 less than 20 (**j**) 6 less than 11
(**k**) 4 less than 16 (**l**) 8 less than 20

3 Make up some "**more**" or "**less**" questions for your neighbour to answer. Make sure you know the answers yourself.

B Going up

You can see that 4 more than 6 is 10.
A short way of saying this is 6 + 4 = 10.

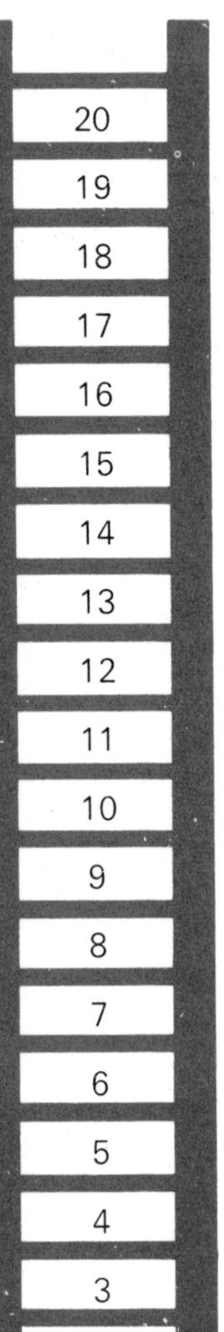

The sign + means add.

1 Write in this short way:

(a) 5 more than 4 is 9 (b) 2 more than 5 is 7
(c) 8 more than 6 is 14 (d) 4 more than 8 is 12
(e) 7 more than 8 is 15 (f) 5 more than 10 is 15
(g) 9 more than 10 is 19 (h) 7 more than 8 is 15

2 Use the ladder to find the missing number:

1	6 + 5 = □	**2**	8 + 4 = □	**3**	7 + 6 = □
4	8 + 7 = □	**5**	9 + 3 = □	**6**	10 + 5 = □
7	7 + 10 = □	**8**	8 + 6 = □	**9**	7 + 8 = □
10	9 + 5 = □	**11**	4 + 7 = □	**12**	9 + 9 = □

Going down

You can see that 3 less than 10 is 7.
The short way of writing this is 10 − 3 = 7.

The sign − means take away.

3 Write in this short way:

(a) 4 less than 9 is 5 (b) 6 less than 11 is 5
(c) 5 less than 20 is 15 (d) 7 less than 16 is 9
(e) 3 less than 18 is 15 (f) 8 less than 20 is 12
(g) 10 less than 19 is 9 (h) 9 less than 15 is 6

4 Find the missing number:

1	9 − 3 = □	**2**	10 − 6 = □	**3**	12 − 4 = □
4	11 − 5 = □	**5**	14 − 4 = □	**6**	15 − 5 = □
7	20 − 5 = □	**8**	11 − 3 = □	**9**	12 − 3 = □
10	20 − 8 = □	**11**	16 − 6 = □	**12**	20 − 6 = □

Looking back

A Write these numbers in figures.

1 Nine
2 Twenty-nine
3 Thirty-four
4 Fifty-six
5 Sixty-seven
6 Seventy-one
7 Ninety-three
8 Eighteen
9 Forty-five
10 Eighty-two
11 Thirteen.
12 Thirty-eight

B Write these numbers in figures.

1 Two more than fourteen.
2 Five more than ten.
3 Three more than twelve.
4 One more than nineteen.
5 Four more than thirteen
6 Ten more than eight.
7 Nine more than ten.
8 Four more than fourteen
9 Six more than nine.
10 Seven more than seven.

C Finding the missing numbers.

1 1 2 3 4 ? 6 7.
2 10 9 8 ? 6 5 ?
3 10 20 30 40 ? 60.
4 2 4 ? 8 10 ?

D Find the number "a" stands for.

1 5 10 15 a 25.
2 1 3 a 7 9.
3 10 8 6 a 2.
4 12 14 a 18 20.

E Put these numbers in order of size with the smallest first.

1 8, 2, 3, 5, 7, 1, 9.
2 13, 15, 12, 18, 17, 14.
3 20, 5, 15, 30, 10, 25.
4 19, 4, 16, 2, 26, 9.
5 28, 23, 3, 27, 15, 8.
6 5, 3, 50, 28, 7, 15.
7 6, 1, 25, 21, 14, 32.

F Write down the number which is :—

1 2 less than 20.
2 5 less than 15.
3 4 less than 14.
4 7 less than 20.
5 6 less than 15.
6 8 less than 19.
7 3 less than 16.
8 9 less than 15.

Addition

G What do these numbers add up to?

1	6 + 6	**6**	8 + 10	**11**	3 + 7 + 5	**16**	4 + 2 + 4
2	8 + 7	**7**	6 + 5	**12**	2 + 8 + 6	**17**	9 + 6 + 1
3	3 + 7	**8**	4 + 9	**13**	7 + 6 + 4	**18**	3 + 5 + 6
4	6 + 8	**9**	8 + 8	**14**	5 + 3 + 2	**19**	2 + 3 + 7
5	10 + 9	**10**	7 + 9	**15**	4 + 8 + 8	**20**	4 + 5 + 5

H Find the missing numbers:

1	1 + ? = 10	**6**	? + 3 = 8	**11**	10 + 5 = ?
2	2 + ? = 10	**7**	? + 5 = 9	**12**	? + 20 = 28
3	6 + ? = 10	**8**	? + 2 = 12	**13**	? + 6 = 11
4	7 + ? = 10	**9**	? + 6 = 16	**14**	10 + 10 = ?
5	5 + ? = 10	**10**	? + 4 = 11	**15**	20 + 10 = ?

You can see that on one branch of the tree there are 5 birds, on another branch 3 birds and on another 4 birds. Altogether there are 5 + 3 + 4 birds = 12 birds. Would it make any difference if we changed the numbers round like this: 4 + 5 + 3? Add and see. Or like this: 3 + 4 + 5? Add and see. Of course, it makes no difference. Sometimes we make adding easier if we change the numbers round. Suppose we want to add 8 + 9 + 2.

If we add 8 and 2 first we get 10. 10 + 9 = 19. Easy, isn't it?

I Change these numbers round to make it easier to add and then add:

1	2 + 6 + 8	**7**	14 + 5 + 6	**13**	11 + 5 + 9
2	7 + 5 + 3	**8**	15 + 8 + 5	**14**	5 + 2 + 8
3	6 + 9 + 4	**9**	16 + 2 + 4	**15**	7 + 6 + 13
4	9 + 8 + 1	**10**	13 + 9 + 7	**16**	8 + 6 + 2
5	2 + 7 + 8	**11**	12 + 6 + 8	**17**	8 + 5 + 15
6	3 + 9 + 7	**12**	5 + 8 + 15	**18**	9 + 8 + 12

Subtraction

The sign — means subtract, or take away

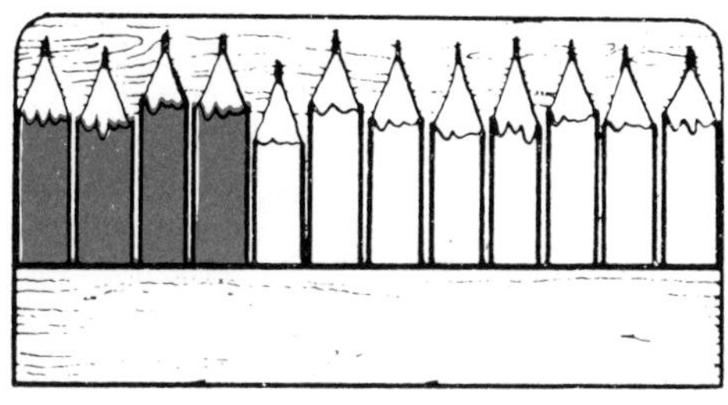

How many pencils are in the box?
If I take away the **coloured** pencils, how many pencils are left in the box?
You could write this in your book like this:

$$12 - 4 = 8$$

J Do these subtractions:

1	10 — 4 =	**5**	10 — 6 =	**9**	20 — 5 =	**13**	20 — 3 =
2	12 — 7 =	**6**	12 — 4 =	**10**	14 — 11 =	**14**	20 — 4 =
3	11 — 5 =	**7**	14 — 10 =	**11**	15 — 9 =	**15**	20 — 7 =
4	11 — 4 =	**8**	15 — 8 =	**12**	16 — 7 =	**16**	20 — 9 =

K **1** Mother bought 12 eggs.
She used 5 of them.
How many had she left?

2 I am 14 years old.
Mary is 6 years younger.
How old is Mary?

3 Tom had 15 marbles
He lost 8 of them.
How many had he left?

4 A grocer had 20 loaves.
He sold 13 of them.
How many had he left?

5 Kate had 16 sweets in her bag.
She gave 5 to Doris.
How many had Kate left?

6 20 boys were playing football in a busy street. 6 ran away when they saw a policeman coming.
How many were left?

7 In a darts game Fred scored 20 points. Jack scored 13. By how many points did Fred win?

8 How many marbles must be taken away from 20 to leave 8?

9 A man bought 18 cigars.
After he had smoked 5, how many were left?

10 In my book there are 20 pages.
I have read 7 pages.
How many have I still to read?

Abacus counting 1 "holes and stones"

Men long ago used to live in caves, or mud huts. They kept sheep or cattle. These they let out to feed on grass during the day, but at night, they kept them inside fences. To see that all the sheep or cattle returned at night, early man, who could not count as you can, used various things to count them as he let them out, and to count them again when they came back at night.

To count his sheep or cattle :

1 he made scratches in the earth.
2 he made knots in grass.
3 he put down rows of nuts or acorns.
4 he put down heaps of grain.
5 he, usually, used pebbles, or shells, or stones.

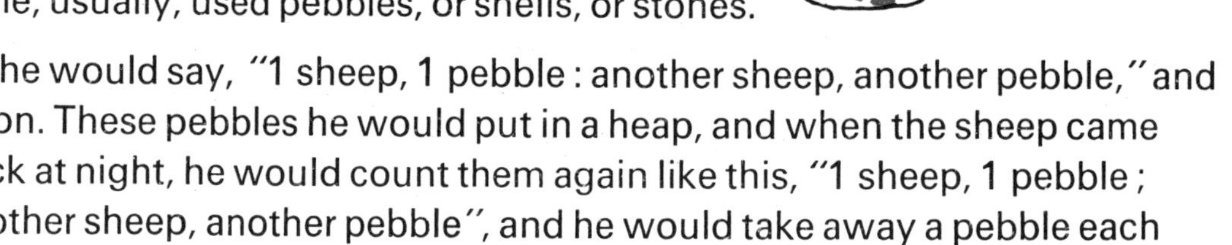

So he would say, "1 sheep, 1 pebble : another sheep, another pebble," and so on. These pebbles he would put in a heap, and when the sheep came back at night, he would count them again like this, "1 sheep, 1 pebble ; another sheep, another pebble", and he would take away a pebble each time a sheep came back.

Suppose one night, this number of sheep came home, and the stones left were like this :

Number Counted

Number Left

How many sheep had still to come home ?

One day, a clever man, who had lots of sheep and found it hard to count so many stones, had a good Idea!
He used larger stones to count as ten, because he had ten fingers. So that every time that ten sheep came in, and he had ten stones in a hole in the ground, or in a heap, he put a larger stone to take the place of the ten small ones, like this:

How many sheep would this stand for?

Later, he would use a larger stone still to stand for ten lots of ten or one hundred (100), a larger one still to stand for ten lots of a hundred (1000).

How many sheep do these stones show?
The small "ones" stones are put into holes coloured **Red.**
And the "tens" stones are put into holes coloured **Light Red.**
The "hundreds" stones are put into holes coloured **Grey.**

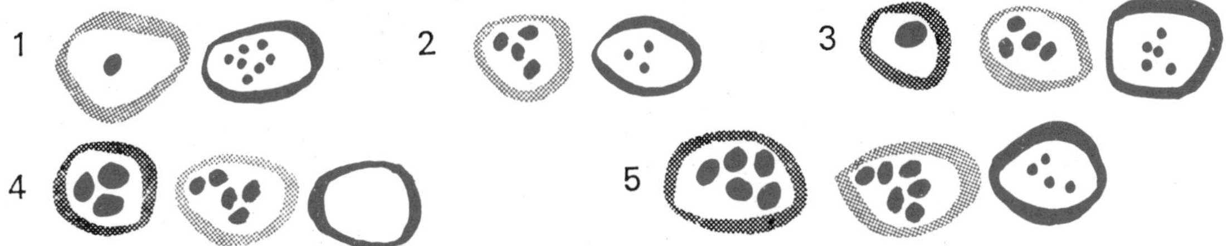

A Write these stone numbers down in our numbers:

1

2

3

4

5

6

7

8

9

10

B Write these down as stone numbers:

1	14	**4**	23	**7**	760	**10**	607
2	45	**5**	65	**8**	500	**11**	204
3	62	**6**	56	**9**	856	**12**	433

Abacus counting 2

The First Abacus

One day a man was using pebbles to count his sheep, when he had an idea. He drew three long scratches in the sand. He put a pebble in the scratch line, or groove, on the right for every sheep. 9 pebbles in this groove meant 9 sheep. When he counted one more sheep, he put 1 pebble in the second groove, and took away the 9 pebbles in the right-hand groove.
His count now looked like this:

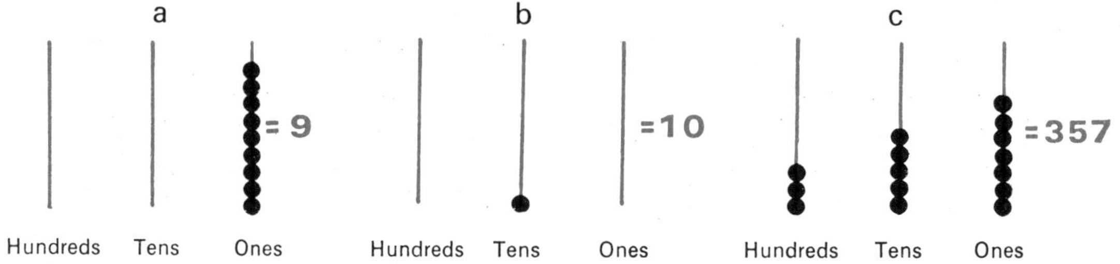

So he had 1 "ten" and no "ones".
Here you can see the number **357** (three hundreds, five tens and seven ones).
Sometimes there was no pebble in a groove:

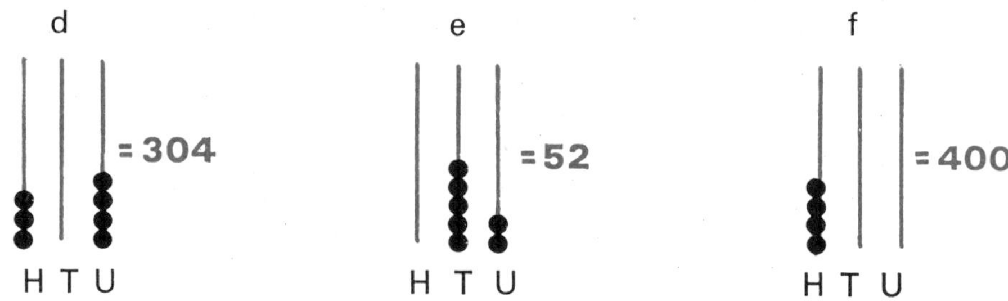

C **Note that**

H is short for hundreds, **T** is short for tens, **U** is short for Units (the "ones").

Here are some abacus numbers. Write them in our numbers.

D

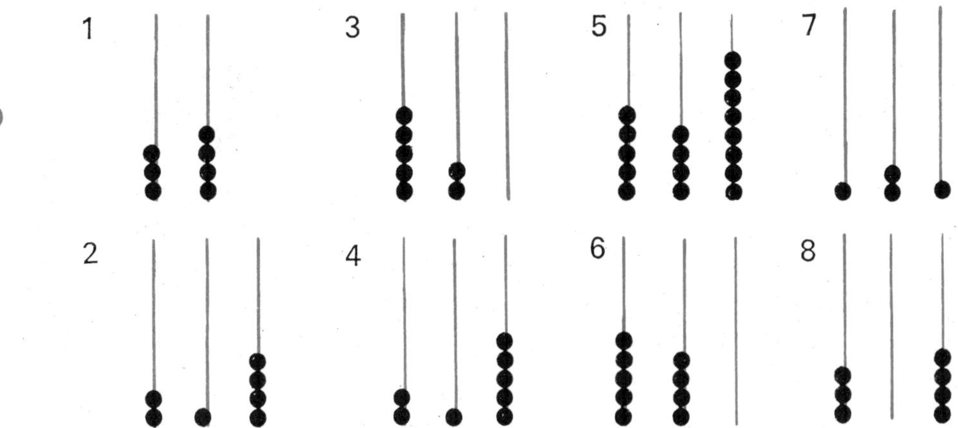

Now draw these numbers as abacus numbers.

18	630	101
245	245	406
566	204	532
408	230	600

Abacus counting 3 addition and subtraction

The abacus is a counting frame. It was used in the times of the Romans and is still used in some countries in the Far East. Instead of grooves or scratches in the sand with pebbles in them, it was easier to count on beads strung on string. Some were used to count in fives and some in tens. Shopkeepers used to count with an abacus in front of them ; so that we now talk about the "counter" in a shop.

You can make an abacus in several ways.
Here are two ways.

A Pegboard and pegs.

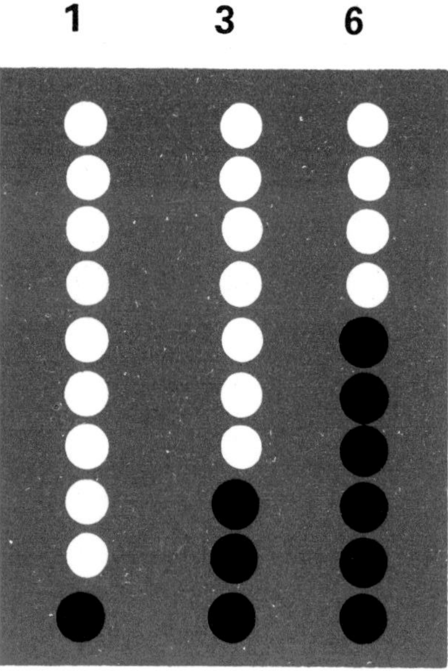

B Cardboard and counters.
Colour the lines.

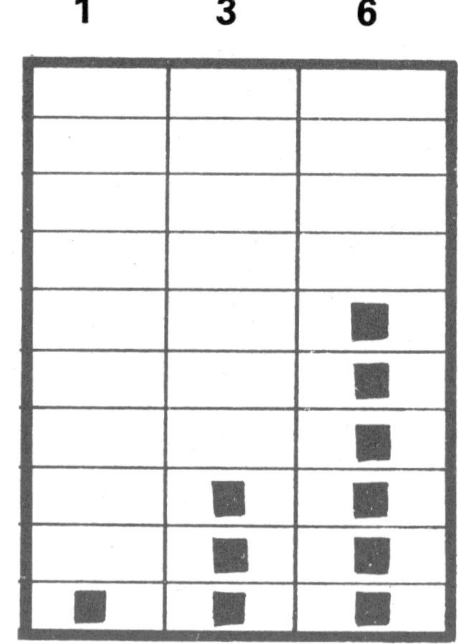

Adding Let's try some adding on the abacus.

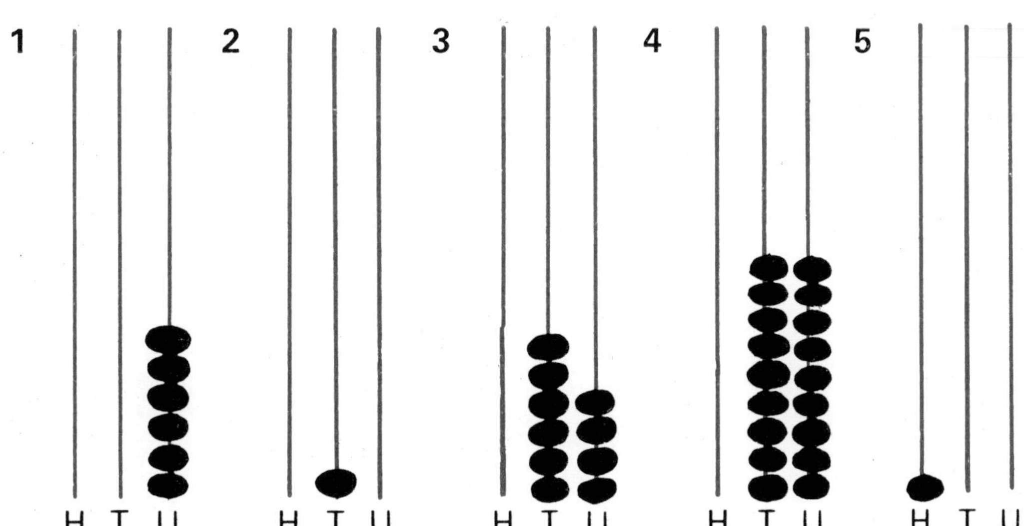

1 Start with 6.

2 If we add 4, we count 6 + 4 = 10 (1 ten and 0 ones). We leave the ones column blank and "carry" or "add" 1 ten to the tens column.

3 Add 54 on (5 tens and 4 ones).
We put another 5 in the tens column and 4 in the ones column. We now have 64.

4 Add 35 on. This makes 99.

5 Now if we add 1 on to 99 (= 100) we get 10 in the ones column, so we add or "carry" one to the tens column and leave the ones column blank. This makes 9 + 1 = 10 in the tens column. So we add 1 to the hundreds column and leave the tens column blank.

Every time the beads or counters add up to ten, we "carry" one and add it to the column on the left.

C Try these on your abacus.

1	7 + 4	**6**	13 + 8	**11**	16 + 5 + 3	**16**	88 + 12 + 7
2	6 + 8	**7**	17 + 5	**12**	18 + 6 + 6	**17**	98 + 2 + 4
3	5 + 5	**8**	15 + 5	**13**	24 + 7 + 5	**18**	100 + 14 + 6
4	9 + 8	**9**	16 + 7	**14**	35 + 6 + 7	**19**	124 + 16 + 8
5	14 + 6	**10**	20 + 8	**15**	75 + 10 + 8	**20**	141 + 19 + 2

Subtracting

Some subtractions are very easy on the abacus.

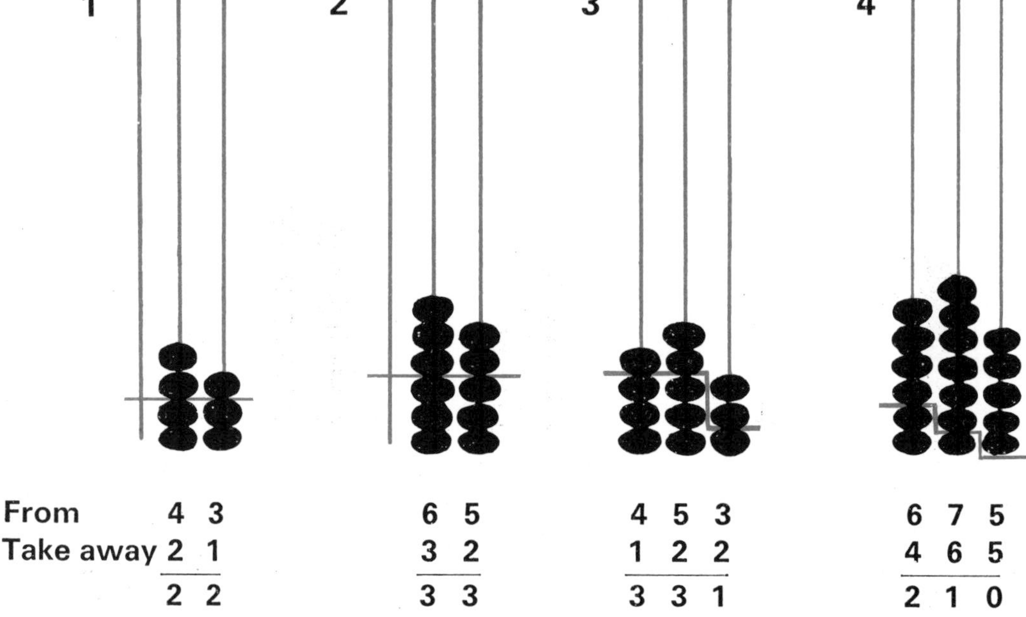

Notice you can test your answer to subtractions by adding your answer to the bottom ("take-away") line. If these add up to the top line, you are right! e.g. 22 + 21 = 43, and so on.

D Try these on your abacus (— means "take away", so 18 — 8 means "From 18 take away 8").

1	15 — 3	**4**	36 — 4	**7**	89—45	**10**	258 — 58
2	18 — 7	**5**	49 — 9	**8**	95 — 64	**11**	274 — 71
3	24 — 3	**6**	85 — 14	**9**	146—36	**12**	344 — 123

Addition and subtraction

Addition

Add (Do these without using the abacus)

A	(a)	(b)	(c)	(d)
1	4 3 6	5 2 7	7 4 5	3 8 5
2	2 8 7	6 3 6	9 3 8	5 6 4
3	7 3 7	6 4 8	3 2 1	9 3 4
4	3 9 5	2 7 6	8 3 6	6 5 3
5	6 7 8	9 5 5	3 9 6	1 8 7

B	(a)	(b)	(c)	(d)
1	12 6 23	14 8 12	3 8 14	15 12 23
2	15 13 12	21 18 23	24 14 23	16 13 34
3	27 18 32	28 26 15	14 27 23	32 17 11
4	19 15 23	30 25 17	26 14 15	35 26 37
5	16 22 35	12 34 26	38 21 36	19 26 34

C 1 Bill had 21 marbles. John gave him 9 more.
How many had he then?

2 What is 15 more than 16?

3 There are 18 people upstairs on a bus. There are 22 downstairs.
How many people are on the bus?

4 In a class there are 26 boys and 18 girls.
How many children are in the class?

5 There are 34 sheep in one field and 28 in another.
How many sheep is this altogether?

D 1 Mary gathered 47 shells, Jane 52 and Kate 28.
How many shells did they gather altogether?

2 John spent 16 pence on Monday, 18 pence on Tuesday and 22 on Wednesday.
How many pence was this altogether?

3 In my garden I have 28 red roses, 16 yellow roses and 17 white roses.
How many roses have I?

4 Tom has 18 marbles and Jim and Fred have 16 each.
How many marbles is this altogether?

5 Mary is 16 years old. Her mother is 29 years older.
How old is Mary's mother?

Subtraction

Subtract (no carrying)

	(a)	(b)	(c)	(d)
E 1	15 −12	54 −32	46 −21	28 −16
2	48 −14	35 −12	36 −11	67 −34
3	64 −32	38 −15	39 −17	58 −23
4	89 −32	74 −21	55 −33	82 −51
5	68 −14	87 −25	93 −23	79 −36
6	879 −243	965 −422	786 −342	684 −213
7	536 −114	698 −235	987 −432	896 −271
8	944 −213	758 −315	649 −213	839 −412

1 A farmer had 84 sheep. He sold 32 of them. How many had he left?

2 There were 36 cherries in a bag. Tom took out 32 of them. How many cherries were left in the bag?

3 A man had 95 hens. He lost 12 of them. How many had he left?

4 A boy had 56 marbles. 32 of them were red and the rest were blue. How many were blue?

5 There are 72 eggs in a box. 30 are sold. How many are left?

6 I take 23 biscuits out of a tin holding 87 biscuits. How many will be left in the tin?

Subtract (with carrying)

	a	b	c	d
1	34 −16	33 −16	32 −19	34 −18
2	42 −16	43 −19	32 −17	44 −18
3	62 −18	62 −14	31 −16	41 −17
4	33 −19	32 −15	46 −18	53 −27
5	82 −18	82 −26	41 −23	53 −19
6	61 −29	72 −36	83 −48	94 −57
7	55 −29	66 −28	74 −29	81 −37
8	70 −25	60 −18	50 −22	90 −38

1 A boy did 24 sums. 9 were wrong. How many were right?

2 There are 60 pages in my book. I have read 32 of them. How many pages have I still to read?

3 86 children went to a Sunday School picnic. 49 were boys. How many girls were there?

4 There were 62 people on a bus. 35 were upstairs. How many were downstairs?

5 How many are left when 27 nuts are taken from 50?

6 A boy pulled 18 cherries from a tree which had 60 cherries on it. How many cherries were left on the tree?

Make your addition and Subtraction table

+ − + − +

Here is an addition table.

Parts of it have been filled in for you.

Can you fill in the rest?

Column

Row

+	0	1	6	3	7	5	2	4	8	11	10	9	12
0	0	1	6	3	7	5	2						
1	1	2	7	4	8	6	3						
6	6	7	12	9	13	11	8				16		
7	7	8	13	10	14	12	9						
4	4	5		7	11	9	6						
5	5												17
2	2												
3	3												
8	8												
11	11								19				
10	10												
9	9	10											
12	12					17							

Start with the 1 row.
Add to 1 each column number.
So your numbers in row 1 will now be 1, 2, 7, 4, 8, 6 - - - - - .

Now go to the 2 row.
Add to 2 each column number.
Your numbers in row 2 will now be 2, 3, 8, 5, 9, 7 - - - - .
Continue like this to the 12 row and so complete the square.

A Things to notice

We know already $4 + 3 = 3 + 4 = 7$.
If we go along the 4 row until we come to the 3 column we find 7. Notice also we can go down the 3 column until we come to the 4 row and we get 7 once again.

Show now that **$5 + 7 = 7 + 5$.**

B We can use this table for subtraction.
Suppose we want to find $7 - 3$. We want to subtract 3. Look along the 3 row until you come to 7. 7 is in the 4 column. So $7 - 3 = 4$.
In the same way $8 - 3 = 5$, $9 - 3 = 6$, and so on.

Now use your tables to do these.

1 $10 - 4$ **2** $11 - 4$ **3** $12 - 4$ **4** $10 - 7$ **5** $10 - 6$

Perhaps you could make up another table like this from 13 to 24 in rows and columns. Then do these:

6 $16 - 4$ **8** $17 - 5$ **10** $20 - 6$ **12** $24 - 11$
7 $14 - 6$ **9** $19 - 9$ **11** $21 - 10$

From your table you can see that
$12 - 5 = 7$ *and* $12 - 7 = 5$ *and* $5 + 7 = 12$

C Filling in the missing numbers:

1 $10 - 4 = ?$ *and* $10 - ? = 4$ *and* $4 + ? = 10$
2 $15 - 8 = ?$ *and* $15 - ? = 8$ *and* $8 + ? = 15$
3 $17 - 9 = ?$ *and* $17 - ? = 9$ *and* $9 + ? = 17$
4 $18 - 11 = ?$ *and* $18 - ? = 11$ *and* $11 + ? = 18$
5 $24 - 13 = ?$ *and* $24 - ? = 13$ *and* $13 + ? = 24$

Box pictures

John, Mary and Tom measured their heights with cartons.
How many cartons high is John?
How high is Mary?
How high is Tom?
How much taller than Tom is John?

We can show this by using match-boxes instead of cartons.
Let us say that the height of the match-box stands for 30 cm.
We can show their heights like this.

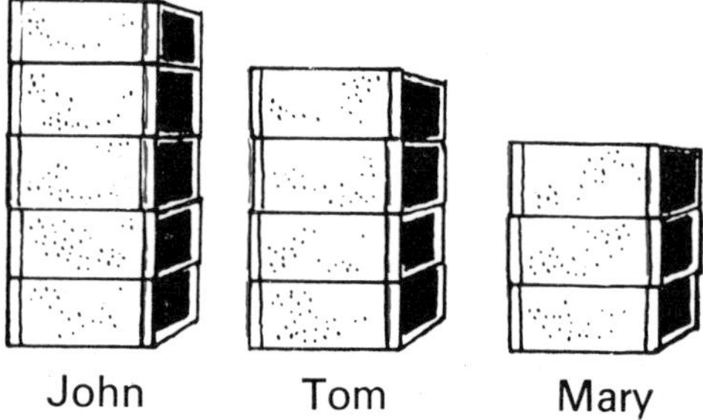

We can make it easier by colouring in squares (as in your exercise-book).

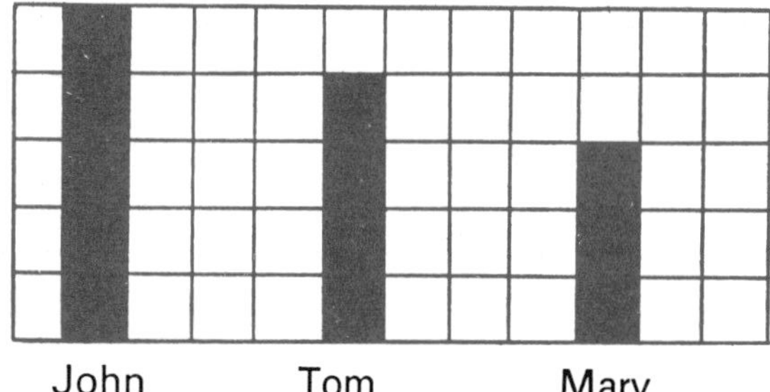

Four girls were given a sweet for every answer they got right.
We could show this with sweets.

Or we can use bobbins or reels of thread, and put M for Mary, J for Jean and so on.

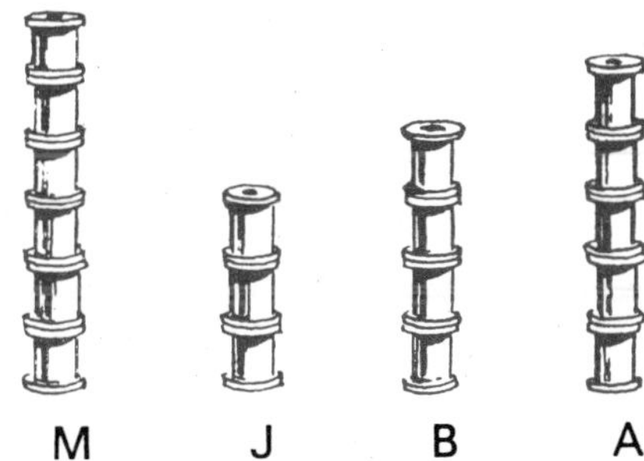

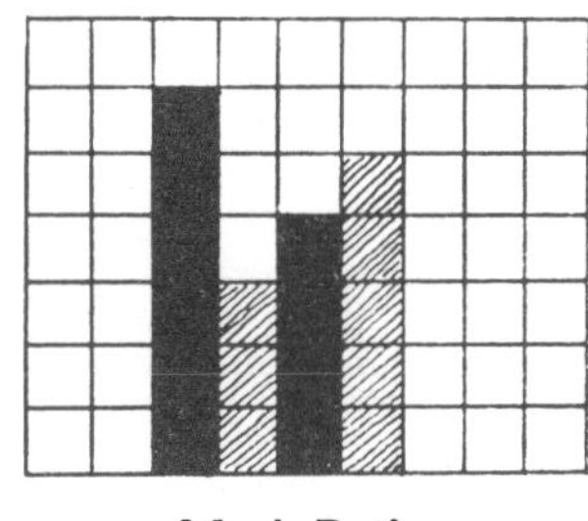

We can use coloured squares. One box means one sweet, and one right answer.

A **1** Who got the most right?
2 How many did Jean get right?
3 How many sweets were given out altogether?

Sometimes we can use little drawings. John, Bill and Tom collect model cars.

John has 6
Bill has 4
Tom has 5

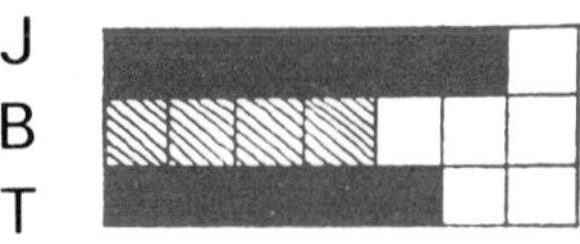

Drawing little cars takes lots of time. We can show the same thing with coloured squares across the page. Each square stands for one car.

Here is a "box picture". It shows the number of goals scored by boys in a football team. Each box stands for one goal.

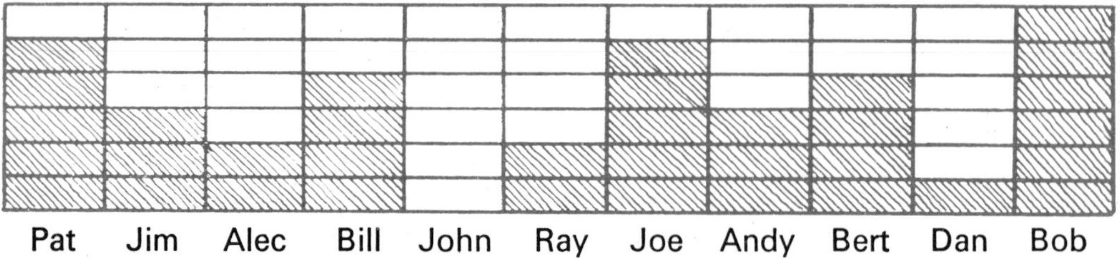

B 1 Who scored the most goals?
2 How many goals did John score?
3 Which players got the same number of goals?
4 How many goals did the team score altogether?
5 Who do you think was the goal-keeper?

C A farmer has 10 hens, 4 ducks, 8 cows, 2 horses, 6 pigs and 9 sheep. Make up a box picture to show this.

D Find out how many different pets your class has—dogs, cats, rabbits, birds and so on. Make a list and then draw a box picture of pets (or use bobbins, counters, pegs on peg board, or match-boxes).

E Make up some more lists, e.g. pocket-money, how far we can jump, scores in a game, the number of dolls each girl has, and so on. Then draw box-pictures to show these.

Counting in twos

A Count in twos up to 20, like this :— 2, 4, 6, 8 - - - - -.

We can show these numbers with coloured counters, or with pegs on a peg board, or with large coloured dots in your exercise book.

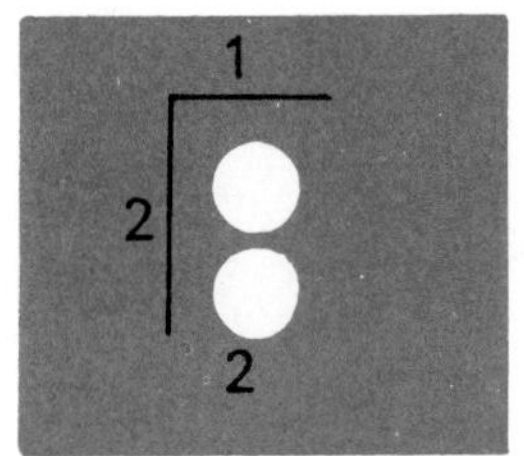

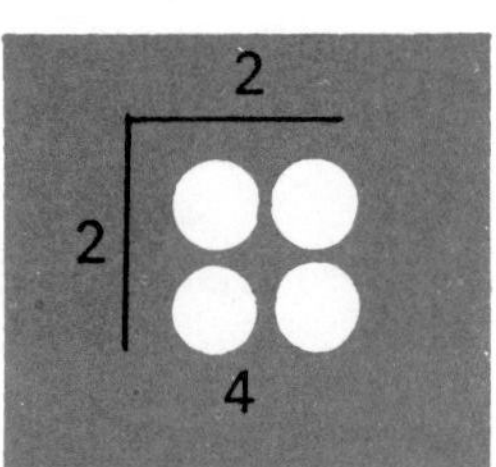

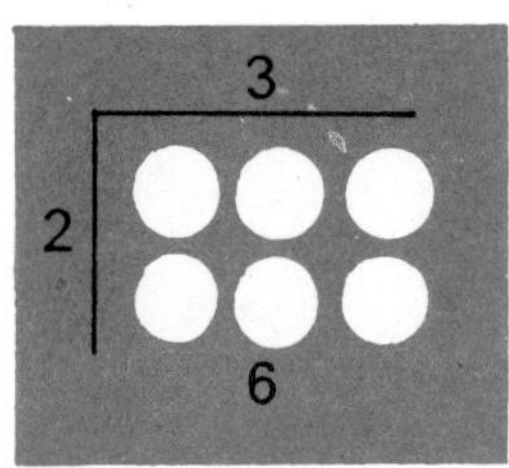

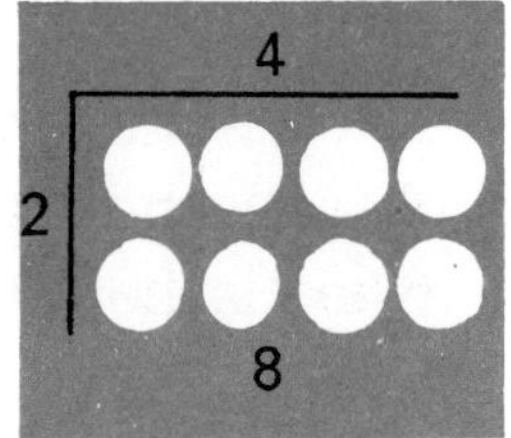

We can see that :

2 ones = 2	2 twos = 4	2 threes = 6	2 fours = 8
or	or	or	or
$1 \times 2 = 2$	$2 \times 2 = 4$	$3 \times 2 = 6$	$4 \times 2 = 8$

× means multiply.

$1 \times 2 = 2$ just means 1 put down 2 times = 2.
$2 \times 2 = 4$ just means 2 put down 2 times = 4.
$3 \times 2 = 6$ just means 3 put down 2 times = 6.
What does 4×2 mean ?

1 Now make up patterns with 2 rows of 5 counters.
Write 2 fives = ? or $5 \times 2 = ?$

2 Do the same with 2 rows of 6 counters, 2 rows of 8 counters, 2 rows of 9 counters, 2 rows of 10 counters.

B Look again at the first pattern. Here we have 2 rows of 1, making 2. But we have also 1 column of 2 counters, making 2. So you can see that 1×2 is the same as 2×1.

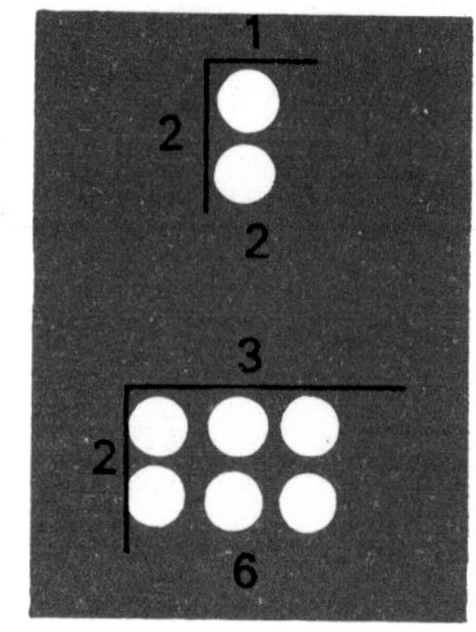

Look at the third pattern. Here we have 2 rows of 3 counters, making 6. But we have also 3 columns of 2 counters, making 6.
So 3×2 is the same as 2×3.

1 Finish these:

4×2 is the same as $\quad \times \quad$.
10×2 is the same as $\quad \times \quad$.
9×2 is the same as $\quad \times \quad$.
8×2 is the same as $\quad \times \quad$.
6×2 is the same as $\quad \times \quad$.
12×2 is the same as $\quad \times \quad$.

2 Write these in your exercise book and put in the missing numbers:

$4 \times 2 =$	$3 \times 2 =$	$6 \times 2 =$
$2 \times 4 =$	$2 \times 3 =$	$2 \times 6 =$
$5 \times 2 =$	$7 \times 2 =$	$8 \times 2 =$
$2 \times 5 =$	$2 \times 7 =$	$2 \times 8 =$
$9 \times 2 =$	$10 \times 2 =$	
$2 \times 9 =$	$2 \times 10 =$	

3 "Double" means two times (or multiply by 2).
Double these numbers:
1, 3, 5, 4, 8, 7, 9, 10.

4 A "pair" means two.
How many shoes in:

2 pairs?	5 pairs?	8 pairs?
3 pairs?	9 pairs?	10 pairs?

5 Twice 4 marbles = 8 marbles.
Twice 5 pencils = ? pencils.
Twice six oranges = ? oranges.
Twice 8 pounds = ? pounds.
Twice 10 pounds = ? pounds.
Twice 7 cows = ? cows.
Twice 9 sheep = ? sheep.
Twice 3 apples = ? apples.

C Multiplication

(no carrying)

	(a)	(b)	(c)	(d)
1	12 × 2	14 × 2	13 × 2	21 × 2
2	22 × 2	23 × 2	24 × 2	32 × 2
3	33 × 2	41 × 2	42 × 2	34 × 2
4	44 × 2	20 × 2	30 × 2	40 × 2
5	231 × 2	342 × 2	413 × 2	142 × 2

(with carrying)

	(a)	(b	(c)	(d)
6	16 × 2	18 × 2	17 × 2	15 × 2
7	27 × 2	26 × 2	28 × 2	25 × 2
8	37 × 2	29 × 2	36 × 2	39 × 2
9	66 × 2	68 × 2	79 × 2	85 × 2
10	87 × 2	78 × 2	86 × 2	89 × 2

D Look back at the patterns.
How many twos make 6 ?
3, of course.
Another way of working this is :

$$6 \div 2 = 3$$

÷ means divided by

Instead of writing "there are 4 twos in 8", we can write

$$8 \div 2 = 4$$

Write these in your exercise book and put in the missing numbers :

1	4 ÷ 2 = ?	**6**	14 ÷ 2 = ?
2	10 ÷ 2 = ?	**7**	20 ÷ 2 = ?
3	12 ÷ 2 = ?	**8**	8 ÷ 2 = ?
4	6 ÷ 2 = ?	**9**	2 ÷ 2 = ?
5	18 ÷ 2 = ?	**10**	16 ÷ 2 = ?

Sometimes when we are dividing things into two equal parts we find we have one thing "left over".
Here are 9 marbles to be divided equally between Jack and Sam.

Jack ● ● ● ●	Sam ● ● ● ●	Left over ●

We can write it in this way : 9 ÷ 2 = 4 R1 (R means "the remainder", or "the bit left over".)

E Now do these:

1	$7 \div 2 =$	**3**	$5 \div 2 =$	**5**	$17 \div 2 =$	**7**	$11 \div 2 =$
2	$3 \div 2 =$	**4**	$9 \div 2 =$	**6**	$19 \div 2 =$	**8**	$21 \div 2 =$

F We put down bigger division like this:

$$\begin{array}{r} 23R1 \\ 2\overline{)47} \end{array}$$

Try these:

	(a)	(b)	(c)	(d)
1	$2\overline{)48}$	$2\overline{)26}$	$2\overline{)42}$	$2\overline{)28}$
2	$2\overline{)68}$	$2\overline{)84}$	$2\overline{)46}$	$2\overline{)82}$
3	$2\overline{)426}$	$2\overline{)648}$	$2\overline{)642}$	$2\overline{)864}$
4	$2\overline{)826}$	$2\overline{)460}$	$2\overline{)680}$	$2\overline{)842}$
5	$2\overline{)43}$	$2\overline{)65}$	$2\overline{)87}$	$2\overline{)29}$
6	$2\overline{)67}$	$2\overline{)89}$	$2\overline{)45}$	$2\overline{)63}$
7	$2\overline{)34}$	$2\overline{)32}$	$2\overline{)38}$	$2\overline{)56}$
8	$2\overline{)65}$	$2\overline{)53}$	$2\overline{)39}$	$2\overline{)35}$
9	$2\overline{)37}$	$2\overline{)51}$	$2\overline{)85}$	$2\overline{)77}$
10	$2\overline{)71}$	$2\overline{)91}$	$2\overline{)95}$	$2\overline{)99}$
11	$2\overline{)492}$	$2\overline{)658}$	$2\overline{)836}$	$2\overline{)294}$
12	$2\overline{)657}$	$2\overline{)433}$	$2\overline{)815}$	$2\overline{)217}$

G Think hard! In some of these you multiply, but in others you divide.

1 I have two boxes. There are 9 pencils in each box. How many pencils have I altogether?

2 If 24 marbles are divided equally between two boys, how many will each get?

3 Mother has two vases. She put 18 roses in each vase. How many roses was this altogether?

4 Two buses took 68 children to the zoo. The same number of children were in each bus. How many were in each bus?

5 A bus can carry 43 people. How many can 2 buses carry?

6 In a country school there are 2 classes. Each class has 27 pupils. How many pupils are there altogether?

7 If I divide 36 pence between two girls, how much money will each girl get?

8 There are 48 pencils in a box. How many pencils are there in 2 boxes?

Straight lines

Tie a weight, like a key, to the end of a piece of string, and hold it like the boy in the picture. The string hangs straight down from the boy's hand. We could also say that it goes straight up from the weight to the boy's hand.

Lines which go straight up and down like this are called **vertical** lines.

Builders use a string with a weight at the end (a "plumb" line) to see if the brick walls are straight up and down (or vertical).

Put some water into a tumbler. No matter how you hold the tumbler the surface of the water is always level.

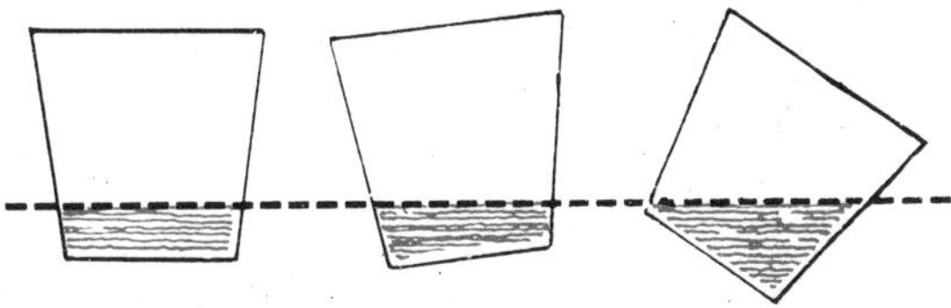

Lines which are level like this are called **horizontal** lines.

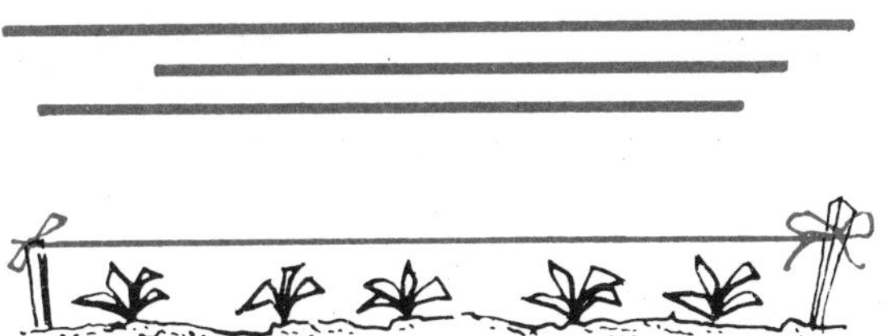

Gardeners and bricklayers often stretch a length of string between two pegs of wood to get a straight horizontal line.

Here are some lines which are neither horizontal nor vertical. They are sloping, or slanting, lines. Another name for a sloping line is an **oblique** line.

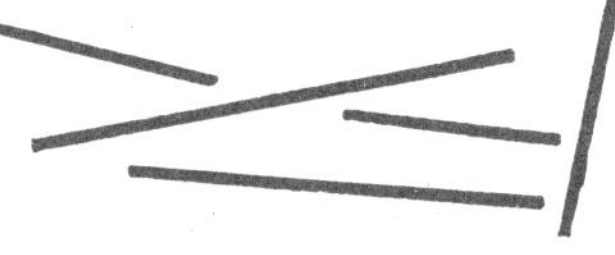

A vertical line is an upright line.
A horizontal line is a level line.
An oblique line is a sloping, or slanting line.

1 2 3

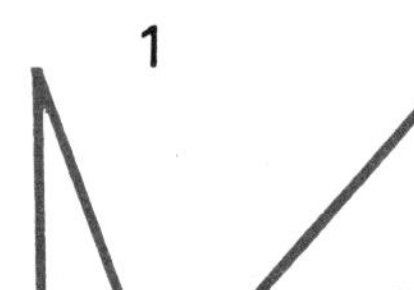

Pick out the vertical, horizontal and oblique lines in these figures.

When a vertical line and a horizontal line meet they make a **Square Corner**. A square corner is also called a **Right Angle**. Every page in this book has four square corners.

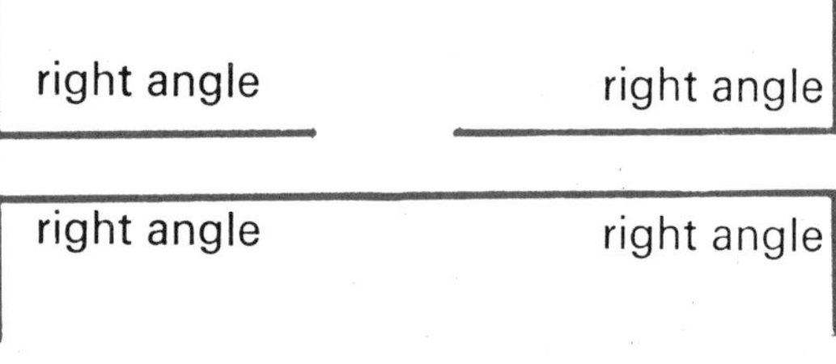

How many square corners can you see in this drawing ?

There are many square corners in your classroom. See how many you can find.

It is a good idea to make a square corner, or right angle, for yourself. Here are two ways of making one.

Get a piece of paper and fold it as shown in these drawings.

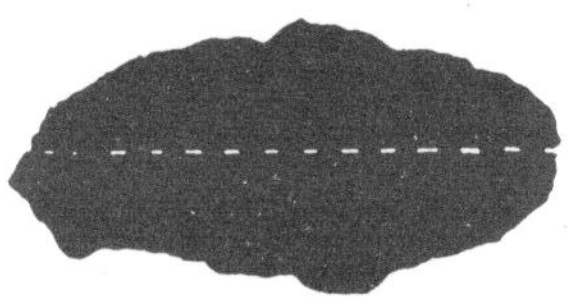

Fold once

Fold over again

Get a coloured circle and fold it twice as shown in the drawings.

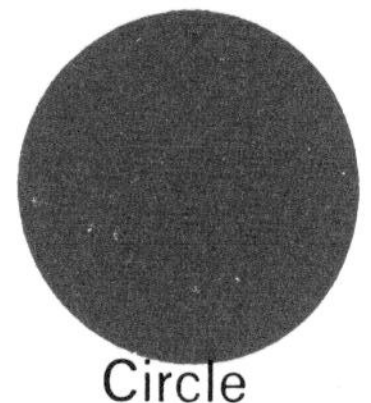

Circle

Fold once

Fold twice

Keep your right angle for testing angles.

A Use your right angle to test these angles. Which of them are right angles?

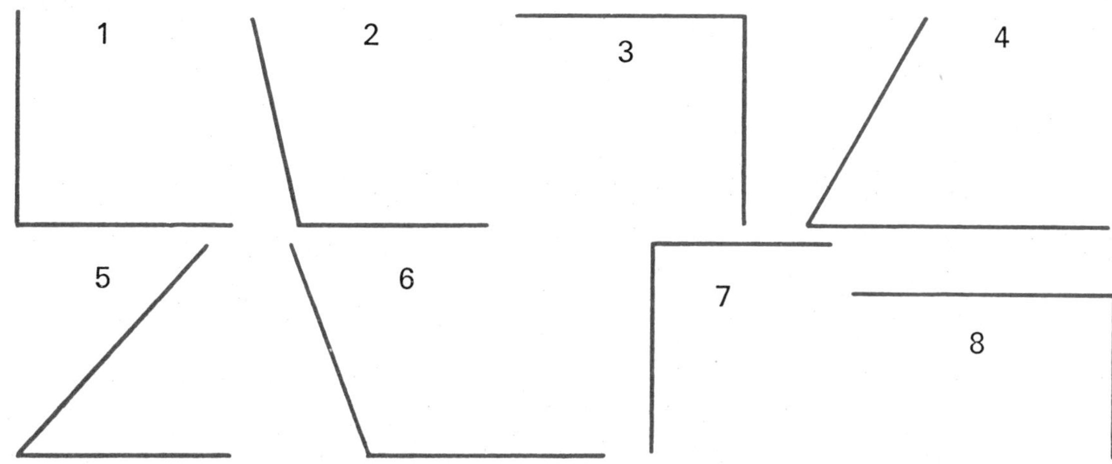

Which of the angles are bigger than right angles?
Which of the angles are smaller than right angles?

B Here are some different shapes. Test the angles with your right angle measure, and see how many right angles there are in each shape.

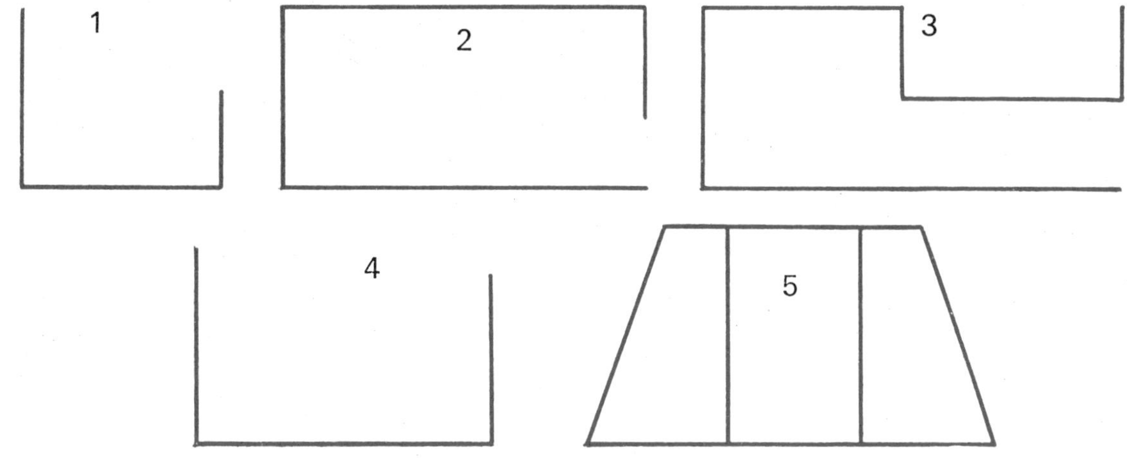

Counting in fours

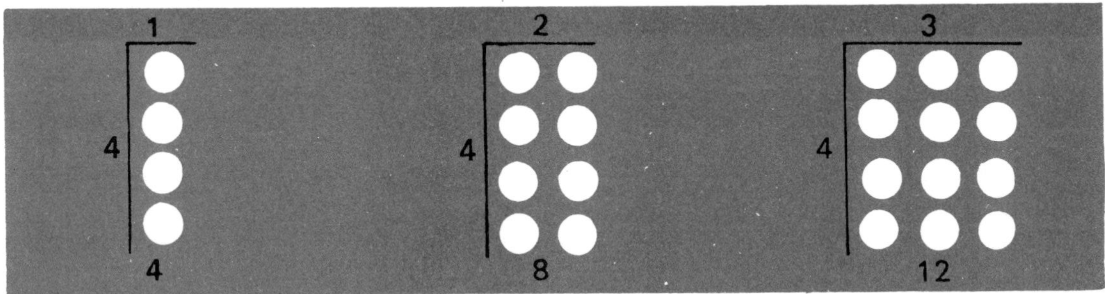

You can see that:

4 ones $= 4$	4 twos $= 8$	4 threes $= 12$
$1 \times 4 = 4$	$2 \times 4 = 8$	$3 \times 4 = 12$
$4 \times 1 = 4$	$4 \times 2 = 8$	$4 \times 3 = 12$
$4 \div 1 = 4$	$8 \div 2 = 4$	$12 \div 3 = 4$
$4 \div 4 = 1$	$8 \div 4 = 2$	$12 \div 4 = 3$

A 1 Make the patterns above with counters or on your peg board and then copy them into your exercise book. Under each pattern write the multiplication and division facts. Learn these facts.

2 Now make the patterns of 4 fours, 4 fives, 4 sixes and so on up to 4 tens. Under each pattern write the multiplication and division facts you discover.

3 Finish these:

(a) 2×4 is the same as . . . . $\times$ . . . .
Each =

(b) 5×4 is the same as . . . . $\times$ . . . .
Each =

(c) 7×4 is the same as . . . . $\times$ . .
Each =

(d) 9×4 is the same as . . . . $\times$ . . . .
Each =

B Multiply:

	(a)	(b)	(c)	(d)
1	12 ×4	16 ×4	17 ×4	18 ×4
2	19 ×4	20 ×4	22 ×4	31 ×4
3	32 ×4	33 ×4	26 ×4	28 ×4
4	29 ×4	34 ×4	37 ×4	23 ×4
5	42 ×4	40 ×4	25 ×4	35 ×4
6	51 ×4	56 ×4	62 ×4	63 ×4

C Divide:

	a	b	c	d
1	4)22	4)28	4)32	4)40
2	4)36	4)48	4)84	4)88
3	4)44	4)96	4)25	4)27
4	4)85	4)52	4)89	4)34
5	4)64	4)67	4)45	4)81
6	4)62	4)68	4)86	4)80
7	4)49	4)56	4)59	4)92
8	4)15	4)47	4)83	4)96

D Think hard! In some of these short stories you should multiply to get the answer, but in others you must divide.

1 A bus can carry 48 people. How many people can 4 buses carry?

2 In a school there are 4 classes. There are 32 children in each class. How many children are there in the school?

3 If I divide 56 sweets among four boys, how many will each boy get?

4 There are 48 chocolates in a box. How many times can I take 4 chocolates from the box?

5 There are 28 lines in each page of my book. How many lines are there in 4 pages?

6 Share 96 nuts equally among 4 boys. How many will each boy get?

7 In a car park there are 4 rows of cars. There are 26 cars in each row. How many cars are in the car park?

8 There are 4 rows of girls. In each row there are 23 girls. How many girls are there altogether?

9 A man earns £88 in 4 weeks. How much does he earn each week?

Money

A Here are the coins we use. They are all new penny coins. A short way of writing new penny is *p*. So 2 new pennies is 2p, and so on.

1. How many new penny coins are there?
2. Which coin has a different shape from the others?
3. What is the shape of the other coins?
4. How many 5p coins are equal to a 10p coin?
5. How many 10p coins are equal to a 50p coin?
6. How many 5p coins are equal to a 50p coin?
7. How many 2p coins are equal to a 10p coin?
8. How many $\frac{1}{2}$p coins are equal to a 2p coin?
9. How many $\frac{1}{2}$p coins are equal to a 5p coin?

B Adding and subtracting new pence

Write the answers to these sums. See how quickly you can do them.

	(a)	(b)	(c)
1	5p + 2p	5p + 2$\frac{1}{2}$p	1$\frac{1}{2}$p + 1$\frac{1}{2}$p
2	10p + 5p	8p + 3$\frac{1}{2}$p	3$\frac{1}{2}$p + 2$\frac{1}{2}$p
3	50p + 5p	10p + 7$\frac{1}{2}$p	4$\frac{1}{2}$p + 5$\frac{1}{2}$p
4	8p + 7p	2$\frac{1}{2}$p + 4p	6$\frac{1}{2}$p + 3$\frac{1}{2}$p
5	9p + 6p	4$\frac{1}{2}$p + 9p	8$\frac{1}{2}$p + 6$\frac{1}{2}$p

	(d)	(e)	(f)
1	5p — 2p	2$\frac{1}{2}$p — 1p	2p — $\frac{1}{2}$p
2	10p — 5p	4$\frac{1}{2}$p — 3p	5p — 1$\frac{1}{2}$p
3	15p — 9p	5$\frac{1}{2}$p — 2p	10p — $\frac{1}{2}$p
4	20p — 10p	8$\frac{1}{2}$p — 3p	10p — 8$\frac{1}{2}$p
5	50p — 5p	14$\frac{1}{2}$p — 7p	7p — 3$\frac{1}{2}$p

 is usually called a FIFTY

 is called a TEN

 is called a FIVE

 is a TWO

 is a ONE

 is a HALF

1 How many FIVES in a TEN?

2 How many TENS in a FIFTY?

3 How many TWOS in a TEN?

4 How many HALVES in a TWO?

Count in tens up to 100—10, 20, and so on.
Do this over and over again until you can do it quickly.
Now count in fives up to 50—5, 10, 15 and so on.

Here is what 3 girls have in their money boxes:

Ella

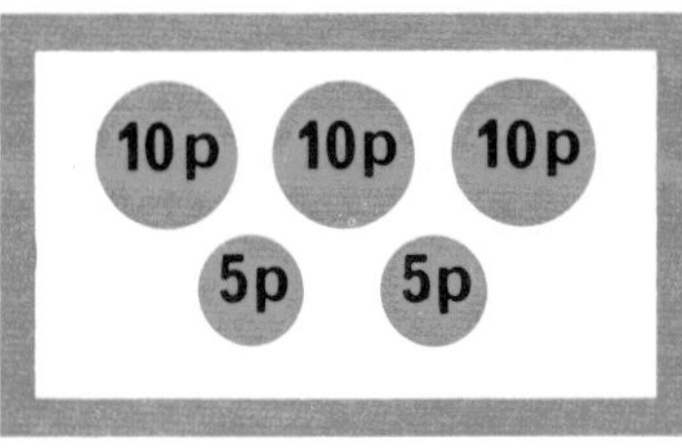

May

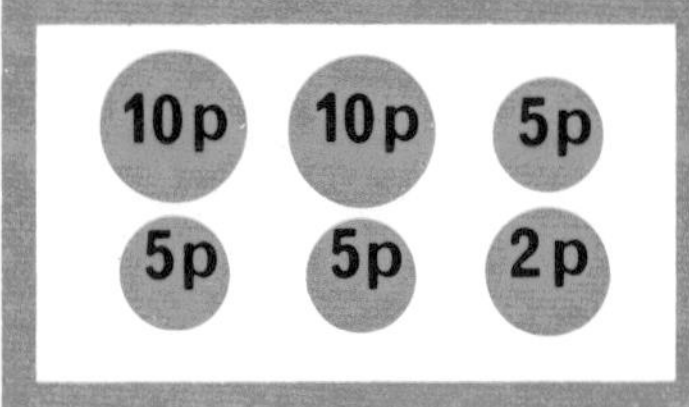

Sue

1 How much money has each girl?
2 Who has the most?
3 Who has the least?
4 How much has Sue more than Ella?
5 How much has Ella more than May?

Here are the prices of some things in a toy shop window.

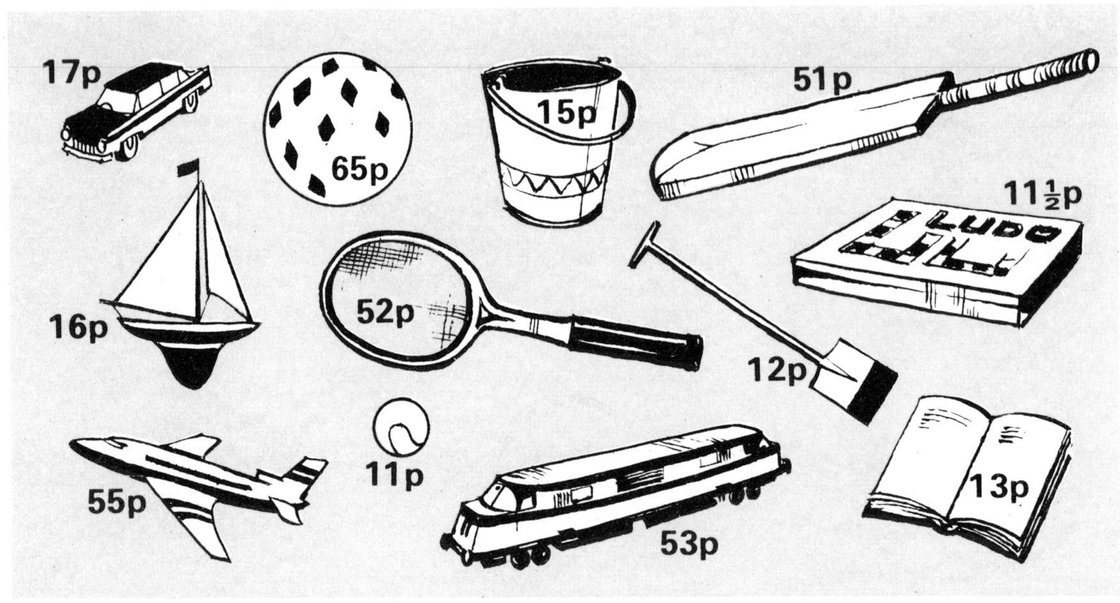

1 You may use real or "pretend" money to help you. Which 2 coins would you use to buy:
(**a**) a pail. (**b**) a spade. (**c**) a tennis ball. (**d**) an aeroplane.
(**e**) a cricket bat. (**f**) a tennis racket?

2 Which 3 coins would you use to buy:
(**a**) a car (**b**) a boat (**c**) a football (**d**) an engine (**e**) a book?

3 Find the cost of:
(**a**) a pail and a spade.
(**b**) a car and a boat.
(**c**) an aeroplane and a car.
(**d**) a football and a book.
(**e**) an engine and a boat.
(**f**) a tennis racket and a tennis ball.
(**g**) a pail, a spade and a book.
(**h**) a football, a boat and Ludo.
(**i**) an engine, a boat and a car.
(**j**) a car, a boat and an aeroplane.
(**k**) Ludo, a car, and a book.
(**l**) a football, a cricket bat and a tennis ball.

4 (**a**) How much more does a pail cost than a spade?
(**b**) How much more does a football cost than a cricket bat?
(**c**) Which 2 things can I buy for exactly 30 pence?
(**d**) How much change would a boy get from 20p after buying a book?

5 How much change should you get from 50p when you spend:
(**a**) 40p, (**b**) 20p, (**c**) 30p, (**d**) 10p, (**e**) 45p, (**f**) 25p, (**g**) 42p, (**h**) 38p, (**i**) 27p, (**j**) 34p, (**k**) 22p, (**l**) 17p?

6 How much change should you get from 100p when you spend:
(**a**) 50p, (**b**) 70p, (**c**) 80p, (**d**) 40p, (**e**) 95p, (**f**) 75p, (**g**) 45p, (**h**) 25p, (**i**) 42p, (**j**) 38p, (**k**) 58p, (**l**) 16p?

D

1 Tom had 5p. He spent $3\frac{1}{2}$p. How much had he left?

2 Jim had 10p. He spent $4\frac{1}{2}$p. How much had he left?

3 Jean had 25p. She spent 6p on chocolate and 5p on sweets.
(**a**) How much did she spend?
(**b**) How much had she left?

4 John had 20p. He spent 9p on comics and 2p on sweets.
(**a**) How much did he spend?
(**b**) How much had he left?

5 Anne went out with 30p. She spent 8p on cakes and 7p on lemonade.
(**a**) How much did she spend?
(**b**) How much had she left?

6 Shirley had 50p. She bought sweets for 12p and biscuits for 9p.
(**a**) How much did she spend?
(**b**) How much had she left?

E

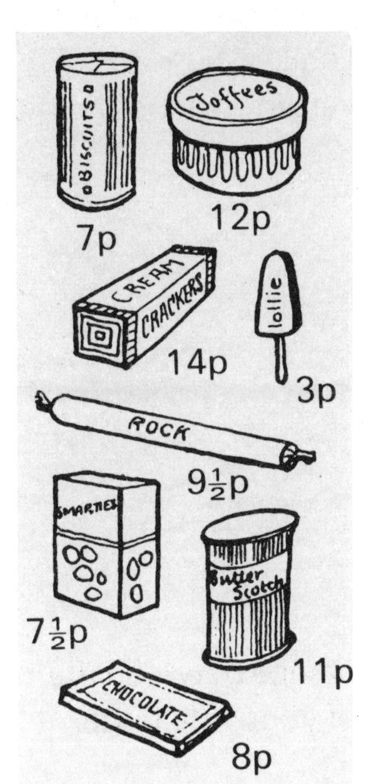

1 I bought a box of Cream Crackers. How much had I left out of 20p?

2 Tom had a 10p coin. He bought a packet of biscuits. How much had he left?

3 Which two things here could I buy for exactly 20p?

4 Which two things could I buy for 15p?

5 Alice bought a packet of biscuits and an ice lollie. How much did she spend altogether?

6 Jim had a 10p coin. He bought a box of Smarties. How much money had he left?

7 How much would I pay for a tin of toffees and a stick of rock?

8 How much would I pay for 2 bars of chocolate?

9 How much less is a packet of biscuits than a box of Cream Crackers?

10 How much more is a stick of rock than a box of Smarties?

Measuring length 1

A **1** Stand with your back to the wall and walk across the room, counting the number of steps you take to reach the opposite wall.
Write in your book :
The room is . . . . . . steps long.

2 In the same way find how many steps the room is wide.
Write in your book :
The room is . . . . . . steps wide.

3 Find how many steps it takes you to walk from one end of the corridor to the other.
Write in your book :
The corridor is . . . . . . steps long.

4 Find how many steps it takes you to walk from one end of the hall to the other.
Find also the number of steps across the hall.
Write the answers in your book.

Can you say why the children don't all get the same answer ?

B Walk heel to toe from the door to the room table or to the teacher's desk and count the number of your foot lengths between them.
Write in your book :
From door to table is . . . . foot lengths.

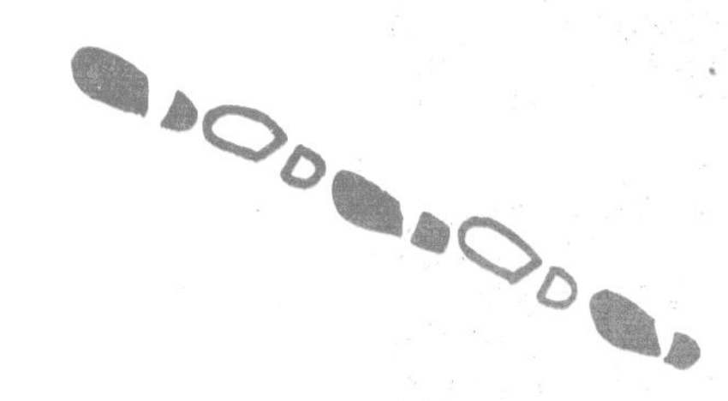

C

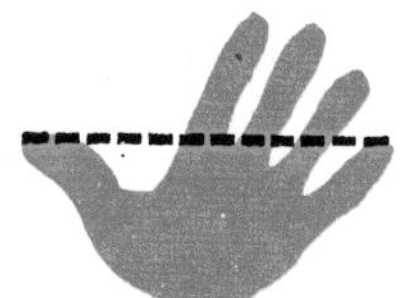

Open your hand wide. The distance between the tip of your thumb and the tip of your little finger is called a **span.**

D 1 See how many spans there are in the length of your desk and in the width of your desk. Write in your book:

> Length of my desk is......spans.
> Width of my desk is......spans.

2 If your teacher found the number of her spans in the length of your desk, would she get a larger number or a smaller number of spans? Why?

If your father has a larger hand than your teacher, would he get more or fewer spans if he measured your desk?

E You can see that we must have a way of measuring which would give us all the same answer.
So we use a measure called a METRE (for short m).
Get a metre stick. You will see it is quite long. It is much longer than your ruler.
Take a good look at the metre stick.

1 **(a)** Now look round the room and name some things which you think are a bit longer than a metre.

(b) Name some things that are not quite as long as a metre. In each case test with the metre stick to see if your guess was a good one.

2 See if you can find anything which you think is just about a metre long or a metre high?

3 Are you a metre tall? Test and see.

4 Is your teacher more than a metre tall? Is she as tall as 2 metres? Test and see.

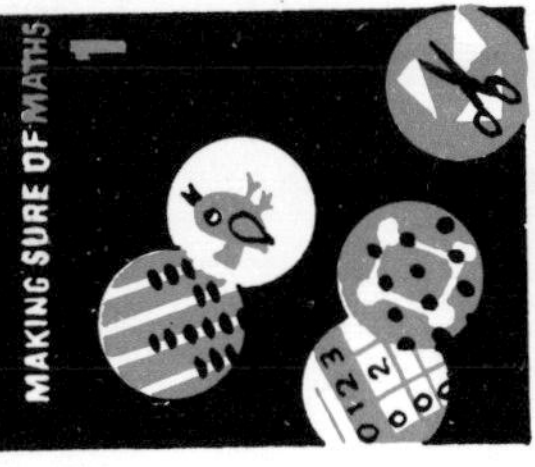

5 Place 4 of these books end to end on a table.
Test their total length with a metre stick.
Is it just a little less or a little more than a metre?

6 Place the metre stick on the floor and mark with chalk a length of 1 metre and another length of 2 metres.

(a) Now say about how many metres long is your room.

(b) About how many metres wide is the room? Test with a metre stick to see if your guess was a good one.

(c) Guess other lengths and then measure them with your metre stick. By doing this many times, you will become quite good at estimating (guessing) lengths in metres.

7 It is a good plan to have a metre measure of your own. Get a piece of string, measure it along a metre stick and cut off 1 metre. You now have a "metre-string" which you can use to measure lengths and heights.

8 Stand facing a wall of your room. Stretch your arms out full length along the wall.

(a) Another pupil should now use a metre stick to see if your "arm stretch" is more or less than a metre.

(b) Find how many of your "arm stretches" are in the length of the wall.

Long lengths can be measured by a trundle-wheel.

The trundle-wheel looks like this. Every time the wheel goes round once you will hear a "click" and you have covered one metre.

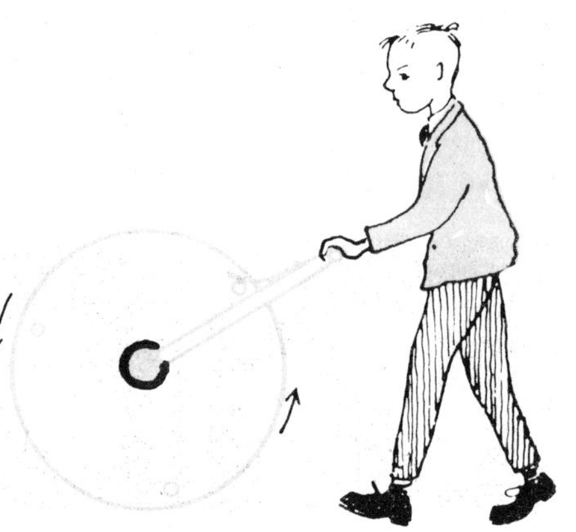

You could measure the length of your playground by "trundling" your wheel and counting the clicks—1 click = 1 metre, 2 clicks = 2 metres and so on.

Table of eights

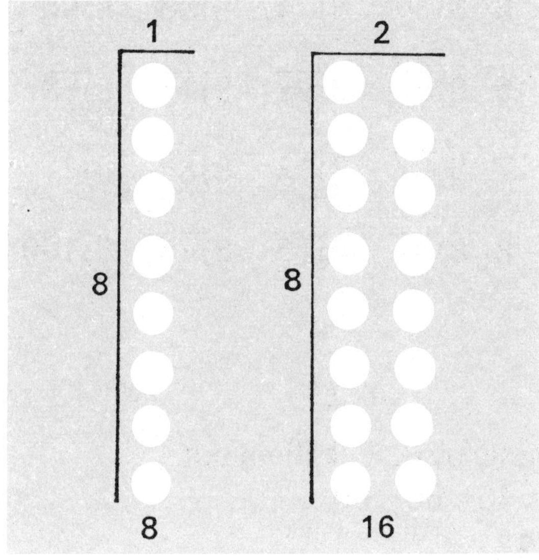

Eight ones = 8
$1 \times 8 = 8$
$8 \times 1 = 8$
$8 \div 8 = 1$
$8 \div 1 = 8$

Eight twos = 16
$2 \times 8 = 16$
$8 \times 2 = 16$
$16 \div 8 = 2$
$16 \div 2 = 8$

A **1** Make these patterns with counters, or on your peg board, and then copy them into your exercise book.
Under each pattern write the multiplication and division facts.
Learn them.

2 Now make the patterns of 8 threes, 8 fours, 8 fives, and so on up to 8 tens. Under each pattern write all the multiplication and division facts you discover.
Learn these facts.

3 How could you use the Table of Fours to make up the Table of Eights?

B Find the missing number:

1	$3 \times 8 = ?$	**6**	$32 \div 8 = ?$
2	$5 \times 8 = ?$	**7**	$40 \div 8 = ?$
3	$6 \times 8 = ?$	**8**	$56 \div 8 = ?$
4	$8 \times 8 = ?$	**9**	$72 \div 8 = ?$
5	$10 \times 8 = ?$	**10**	$80 \div 8 = ?$

C If "**a**" stands for the missing number, find what "**a**" is.

1	$a \times 8 = 16$	**6**	$24 \div 8 = a$
2	$a \times 8 = 32$	**7**	$48 \div 8 = a$
3	$a \times 8 = 72$	**8**	$a = 72 \div 8$
4	$a \times 8 = 64$	**9**	$a = 16 \div 8$
5	$a \times 8 = 80$	**10**	$a = 56 \div 8$

D Multiply:

	(a)	(b)	(c)	(d)
1	14 × 8	17 × 8	15 × 8	19 × 8
2	21 × 8	23 × 8	26 × 8	28 × 8
3	32 × 8	35 × 8	41 × 8	46 × 8
4	27 × 8	43 × 8	18 × 8	36 × 8
5	20 × 8	30 × 8	40 × 8	50 × 8
6	24 × 8	13 × 8	33 × 8	29 × 8

E Divide:

	(a)	(b)	(c	(d)
1	8)32	8)35	8)41	8)45
2	8)50	8)27	8)20	8)80
3	8)37	8)64	8)68	8)76
4	8)19	8)38	8)56	8)60
5	8)30	8)74	8)88	8)90
6	8)96	8)82	8)17	8)59
7	8)87	8)13	8)86	8)71
8	8)31	8)15	8)75	8)100

F **1** Only three of these numbers divide evenly by 8. Pick them out:

24 19 25 32 45 56 60.

2 How many groups of 8 are there in 72?

3 What is the answer when you multiply 5 by 8 and then add 9?

4 How many children are there in a school which has 8 classes with 30 children in each class?

5 How many eggs are there in 8 boxes, if there are 9 in each box?

6 What are the next three numbers in this series?

8, 16, 24, 32, , , .

7 What is the answer when you divide 72 by 8 and then add 6?

8 12 pennies are given to each of 8 boys. How many pennies are there altogether?

Your multiplication square 1

You have already made up an addition square (Page 20). Now you can make up a multiplication square with the table of twos, and the table of fours.

Column

	×	0	1	2	3	4	5	6	7	8	9	10
	0	0	0	0	0	0	0	0	0	0	0	0
	1	0		2		4						
	2	0	2	4	6	8	10	12	14	16	18	20
	3	0		6		12						
Row	**4**	0	4	8	12	16	20	24	28	32	36	40
	5	0		10		20						
	6	0		12		24						
	7	0		14		28						
	8	0		16		32						
	9	0		18		36						
	10	0		20		40						

Draw your square like the one above. We can fill in the 2 Column like this :—
Put down 2 in the 1 Row.
Keep adding twos down the column as shown in the square.
We saw that 2 × 1 is the same as 1 × 2. So we can fill in the 2 Row across the square as shown.
We can now fill in the 4 Column and the 4 Row by adding fours.

In the same way we can put in the table of eights. Start with the 1 Row and the 8 Column by putting down 8. Keep on adding 8 each time down the 8 Column and across the 8 Row.

Notice we can make up the table of fours by doubling the table of twos. We can also make up the table of eights by doubling the table of fours.

You will be able to fill in more of the table after we have had a look at the table of threes, the table of fives—and so on.

A Try these from your table.

1	2×4	**6**	4×3	**11**	8×3	**16**	8×4
2	2×5	**7**	3×4	**12**	8×5	**17**	4×8
3	5×2	**8**	4×6	**13**	8×6	**18**	2×10
4	2×6	**9**	4×8	**14**	7×8	**19**	10×4
5	2×7	**10**	4×7	**15**	8×9	**20**	8×10

We used our addition square for subtractions.
We can use our multiplication square for division.

Suppose we want to find $12 \div 2$.
We want to divide by 2.
Look **along** the 2 row until you come to 12. This comes in the 6 column.
So $12 \div 2 = 6$.

We could also find the answer in this way:—
We want to divide by 2.
Look **down** the 2 column until you come to 12. This comes in the 6 row.
So $12 \div 2 = 6$.

It doesn't matter if we take Row and Column or Column and then Row.

B Now try these from your table.

1	$6 \div 2$	**6**	$8 \div 4$	**11**	$16 \div 8$	**16**	$40 \div 4$
2	$10 \div 2$	**7**	$12 \div 4$	**12**	$24 \div 8$	**17**	$20 \div 4$
3	$14 \div 2$	**8**	$16 \div 4$	**13**	$32 \div 8$	**18**	$72 \div 8$
4	$18 \div 2$	**9**	$24 \div 4$	**14**	$56 \div 8$	**19**	$80 \div 8$
5	$20 \div 2$	**10**	$36 \div 4$	**15**	$64 \div 8$	**20**	$28 \div 4$.

C Some of you may see that we have already filled in small parts of other tables.

Try these "other table" ones.

1	3 × 2	**7**	5 × 2	**13**	6 × 2	**19**	7 × 2	**25**	9 × 2
2	3 × 4	**8**	5 × 4	**14**	6 × 4	**20**	7 × 4	**26**	9 × 4
3	3 × 8	**9**	5 × 8	**15**	6 × 8	**21**	7 × 8	**27**	9 × 8
4	6 ÷ 3	**10**	10 ÷ 5	**16**	12 ÷ 6	**22**	14 ÷ 7		
5	12 ÷ 3	**11**	20 ÷ 5	**17**	24 ÷ 6	**23**	28 ÷ 7		
6	24 ÷ 3	**12**	40 ÷ 5	**18**	48 ÷ 6	**24**	56 ÷ 7		

Keep your square, so that you can fill in more tables later.

D Look at these numbers:

2 3 5 6 8 11 12 14 15 16

1 Which of these numbers are in the table of twos?
2 Which numbers are in the table of fours?
3 Which numbers are in the table of eights?
4 Which numbers are in both the table of twos and the table of fours?
5 Which numbers are in all three tables?

Find as many numbers as you can which can be divided by 2 and 4 and 8.
For example, 32 can be divided by 2, 4 and 8.

Take 4 blocks and arrange them like this.
You can see that we have
2 times 2 blocks = 4 blocks.

Now place another four blocks on top of these.
We have 2 times 4 blocks = 8 blocks.

Add another layer of 4 blocks.
We have 3 times 4 blocks = 12 blocks.
Or we have 2 lots of 6 blocks = 12 blocks.

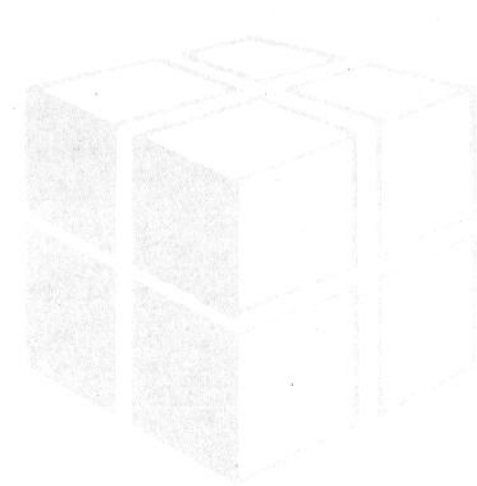

Add more layers of blocks and write down multiplication facts about them.

Measuring length 2

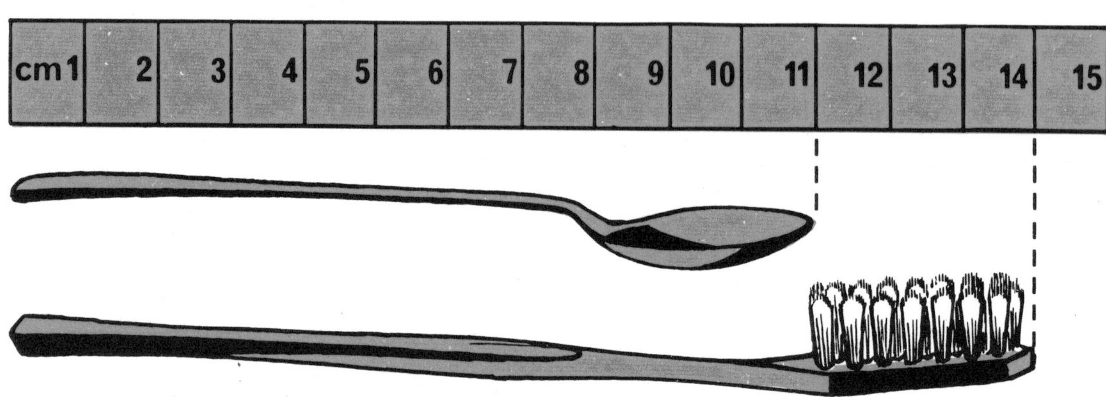

You can see that a metre is too long to measure the length of a postcard, or this book, or your foot.
So we need a smaller measure.
If you look carefully at a metre stick you will find it is divided into 100 smaller parts.
Each of these smaller parts is called a CENTIMETRE (for short **cm**).

1 METRE = 100 CENTIMETRES

A **1** The picture at the top of the page shows a ruler marked in centimetres (cm).

(**a**) How many centimetres long is the ruler?

(**b**) How many centimetres long are the spoon and the tooth brush?

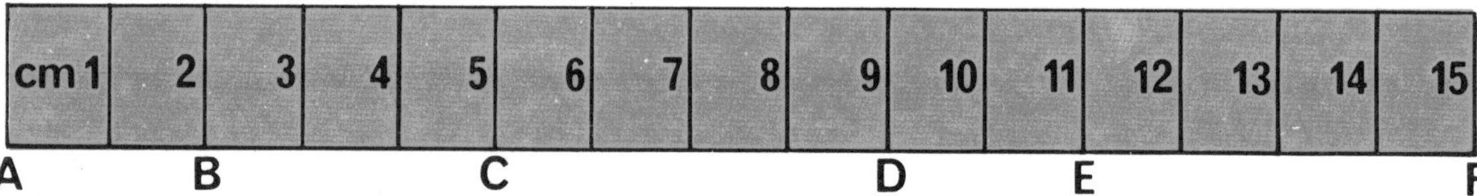

2 How many centimetres are there from:

(**a**) A to B (**b**) A to C (**c**) A to E (**d**) B to C

(**e**) B to D (**f**) C to E (**g**) C to F (**h**) D to F?

3 Use a ruler marked in cm to find the number of cm in these lines.

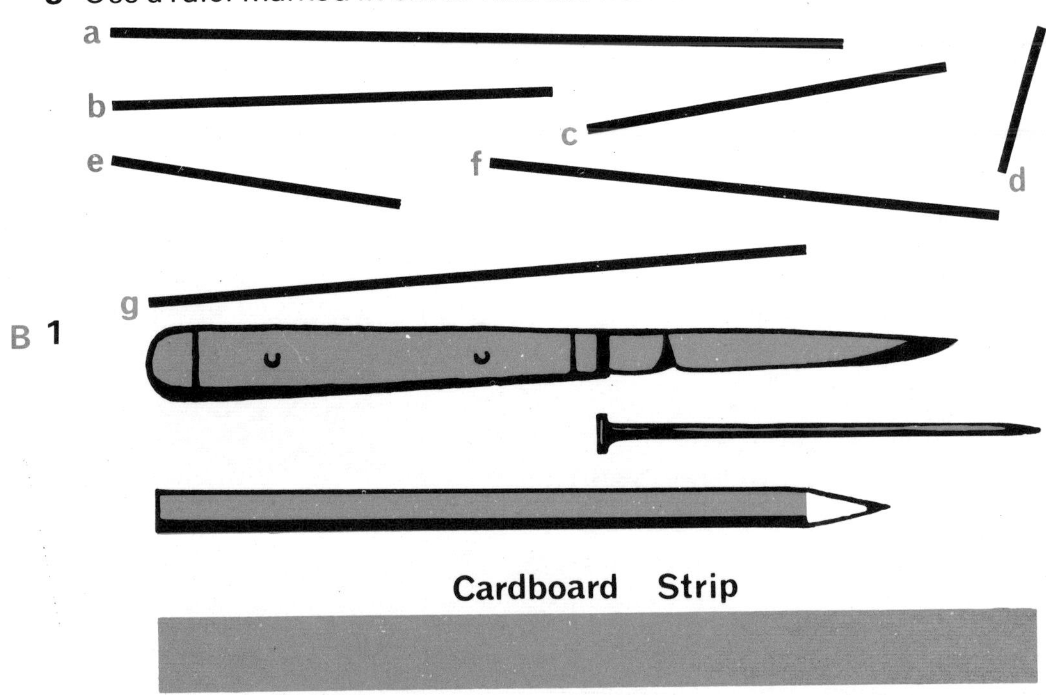

B **1**

Measure the length of the cardboard strip.
Now guess the length of the pencil, the nail, and the knife.
Measure them with your ruler to see if you guessed well.
Guess the length of your own pencil and then measure it.

2 (**a**)
(**b**)
(**c**)
(**d**)
(**e**)

Measure line (**e**) in centimetres.
Guess the lengths of the other lines.
Now measure them to see if you guessed well.

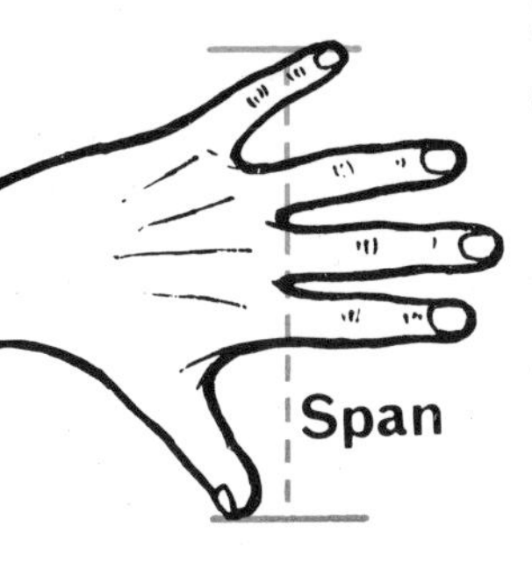

3 Open your hand as wide as you can and place it on a piece of paper. Mark your span, as shown in the drawing. Measure the distance between the marks as close as you can. This will give you the length of your span.
Now write in your book:
The length of my span is about . . . . . . cm.
The length of my desk is about . . . . . . spans, or about . . . . . . cm.
The width of my desk is about . . . . . . spans, or about . . . . . . cm.

4

b c

a

How many centimetres are there in sides a, b and c?
How much longer is side c than side b?
What is the length all round the shape?

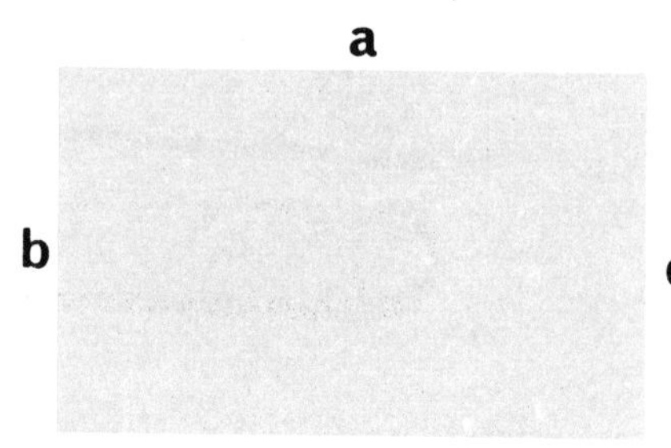

5 Measure the lengths of sides a, b, c and d in this drawing.
What do you find about sides a and c?
What do you find about sides b and d?
How much longer is side a than side b?
What is the distance all round the shape?

6

a

b d

c

(a) How many cm are there in each side?

Write: side a = ... cm
side b = ... cm.
side c = ... cm.
side d = ... cm.

(b) What is the distance all round the shape?

(c) How much longer is side c than side a?

(d) How much longer is side a than side d?

(e) How much longer is side d than side b?

4 Make chalk marks on the floor at your heel and toe.
Measure the length between the marks.
This will give you the length of your foot.

Now walk from heel-to-toe to find the number of foot lengths in the length of the teacher's table, in the width of the door, in the length of a cupboard, and so on.
Write what you find in a table like this:

Table	about . . . . . . foot lengths, or about . . . . . . cm
Door	about . . . . . . foot lengths, or about . . . . . . cm
Cupboard	about . . . . . . foot lengths, or about . . . . . . cm

C Here is how to draw a line 8 cm long:

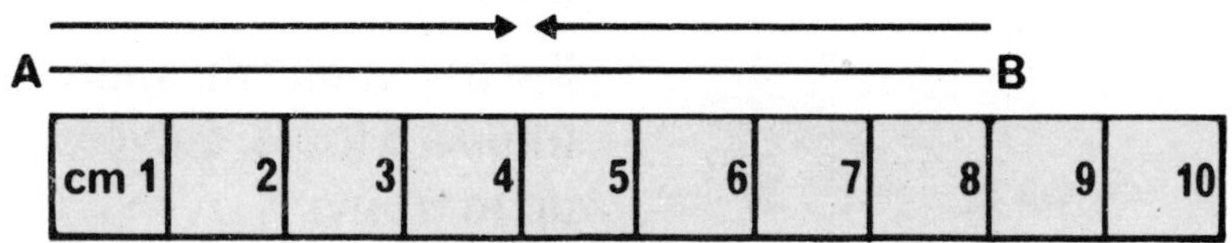

Put your pencil at point A which is the beginning of the ruler.
Draw a line a little way towards point B, as shown by the first arrow.
Now put your pencil at point B and draw another line to meet your first line, as shown by the second arrow.
You will now have drawn a line 8 cm long.
Draw lines of these lengths:
5 cm   7 cm   6 cm   3 cm   9 cm   10 cm

D **1** Would you measure these in metres or in centimetres:
(**a**) this book   (**b**) your desk   (**c**) the school hall
(**d**) the playground   (**e**) a scarf   (**f**) a postcard
(**g**) a football field   (**h**) a street   (**i**) a knife?

2 Make a list of other things you would measure in metres, and a list of things you would measure in centimetres.

Table of fives

A

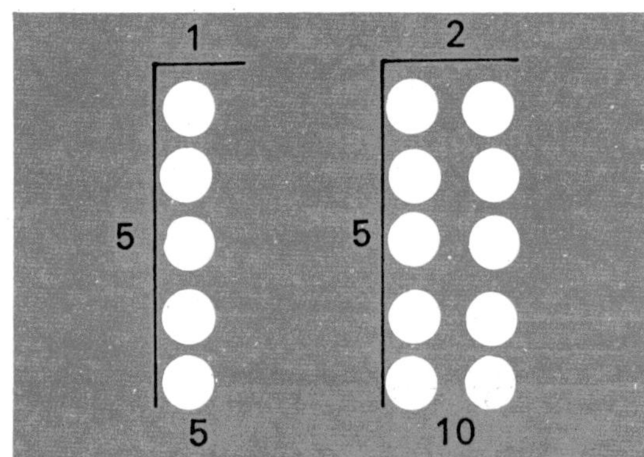

5 ones = 5	5 twos = 10
1 × 5 = 5	2 × 5 = 10
5 × 1 = 5	5 × 2 = 10
5 ÷ 1 = 5	10 ÷ 5 = 2
5 ÷ 5 = 1	10 ÷ 2 = 5

1 Make these patterns with counters or on your peg board and then copy them into your exercise book. Under each pattern write the multiplication and division facts.

2 Now make the patterns of 5 threes, 5 fours, 5 fives, and so on up to 5 tens.
Under each pattern write the multiplication and division facts you discover.

3 Write the Table of Fives in your Multiplication Square.

B If the letter **n** stands for the missing number, find what **n** is.

1	n = 6 × 5	**5**	n = 10 × 5	**9**	n = 45 ÷ 5	**13**	35 ÷ 5 = n
2	n = 9 × 5	**6**	n = 8 × 5	**10**	n = 50 ÷ 5	**14**	15 ÷ 5 = n
3	n = 7 × 5	**7**	n = 20 ÷ 5	**11**	n = 25 ÷ 5	**15**	20 ÷ 5 = n
4	n = 3 × 5	**8**	n = 35 ÷ 5	**12**	30 ÷ 5 = n	**16**	5 × n = 45

C

	(a)	(b)	(c)	(d)
1	12 × 5	15 × 5	21 × 5	24 × 5
2	36 × 5	34 × 5	25 × 5	37 × 5

	(a)	(b)	(c)	(d)
3	41 × 5	45 × 5	53 × 5	28 × 5
4	5)37	5)49	5)60	5)65
5	5)75	5)85	5)95	5)90
6	5)61	5)72	5)43	5)57

D **1** Begin at 5 and count in fives up to 60.

2 Begin at 40 and count backwards in fives.

3 Tom is 9 years old. His mother is 5 times as old as Tom. How old is she ?

4 How many times can I take 5 nuts from a bag holding 35 nuts ?

5 What is 5 times 19 ?

6 There are 52 weeks in a year. How many weeks in 5 years ?

7 How many times can a woman take 5 eggs from a basket holding 60 eggs ?

8 Share 50 sweets equally among 5 girls. How many will each girl get ?

9 3 boys and 2 girls each saved 90 pence for their holidays. How many pence was this altogether ?

10 A bus has seats for 46 people. How many seats will there be in 5 such buses ?

11 A coalman sells 72 bags of coal every day. How many bags does he sell in 5 days ?

12 How many fives are there in 200 ?

E **1** How many groups of 5 are there in 75 ?

2 There are 100 new pence in 1 pound. How many new pence are there in 5 pounds ?

3 Four of these numbers do not divide evenly by 5. Pick them out :

15 20 36 40 46 52 55 59

4 What number does **y** stand for, if **y** = (25 ÷ 5) + 7 ?

5 What is (9 × 5) — 4 ?

6 Write down the next three numbers in this series :

10, 15, 20, 25, ..., ..., ...

Table of tens

1 Without getting any help, see if you can fill in the 10 Column and the 10 Row in your Multiplication Squares.
Some of the squares you have already filled up will help you.

2 Now write the Table of Tens up to 10 times 10 in your exercise book in this way:—

$1 \times 10 = 10$	$10 \times 1 = 10$	$10 \div 10 = 1$
$2 \times 10 = 20$	$10 \times 2 = 20$	$20 \div 10 = 2$
$3 \times 10 = 30$	$10 \times 3 = 30$	$30 \div 10 = 3$

3 If y stands for the missing number, find what y is.

(**a**) $y = 3 \times 10$	(**e**) $y = 8 \times 10$	(**i**) $y = 20 \div 10$
(**b**) $y = 5 \times 10$	(**f**) $4 \times 10 = y$	(**j**) $y = 50 \div 10$
(**c**) $y = 6 \times 10$	(**g**) $7 \times 10 = y$	(**k**) $y = 70 \div 10$
(**d**) $y = 9 \times 10$	(**h**) $10 \times 10 = y$	(**l**) $y = 90 \div 10$

4 Do these:

(**a**) $(6 \times 10) + 5$	(**g**) $(7 \times 10) - (100 \div 10)$
(**b**) $(9 \times 10) + 2$	(**h**) $(4 \times 10) - (90 \div 10)$
(**c**) $(8 \times 10) - 6$	(**i**) $(80 \div 10) + (2 \times 10)$
(**d**) $(7 \times 10) - 9$	(**j**) $(60 \div 10) + (4 \times 10)$
(**e**) $(40 \div 10) + (30 \div 10)$	(**k**) $(90 \div 10) + (3 \times 10)$
(**f**) $(50 \div 10) + (6 \times 10)$	(**l**) $(5 \times 10) + (70 \div 10)$

1 Share 35 sweets equally among 10 boys and keep the rest to yourself.

a) How many does each boy get? **b**) How many do you get?

2 There are 10 rows of chairs in a hall. Altogether there are 90 chairs.
How many chairs are there in each row?

3 I gave 8 boys 10 sweets each and I had 9 left. How many had I to start with?

4 How many times can I take 10 sweets from a box which holds 78 sweets, and how many will be left in the box?

5 There are 10 classes in Workhard School. Each class has 42 children. How many children are there altogether?

6 There are 11 rows of cars in a car park. In each of the first 10 rows there are 14 cars and in the eleventh row there are 12 cars. How many cars are there in the car park?

7 In a bookshop there are 11 shelves. On each of the first 10 shelves there are 26 books and on the eleventh shelf there are 14 books. How many books are there altogether?

8 A box can hold 10 footballs. How many boxes would be needed for 68 footballs?

9 How many tens are there in:
(**a**) 80 (**b**) 100 (**c**) 140
(**d**) 170 (**e**) 200?

10 Add $28 + 15 + 32 + 25$ and divide your answer by 10.

C

1 Which of these numbers divide evenly by 10?
45 50 84 96 100 120

2 **a**, **b** and **c** stand for 3 numbers.
What are they?
70 80 a 100 b c 130

3 If $n = (7 \times 10) + (2 \times 10)$, find what number n stands for.

4 $b = (2 \times 10) - (90 \div 10)$.
Find what **b** stands for.

5 Multiply 9 by 10 and add 8.

6 A farmer has 120 eggs and 10 boxes to put them in. How many should he put in each box?

7 How many times can 10 be taken from 80?

8 What are the missing signs?
(**a**) 140 10 = 14
(**b**) 19 10 = 190
(**c**) 14 10 = 24
(**d**) 96 10 = 86

More money

A Here is what 3 boys have in their money boxes.

Jim

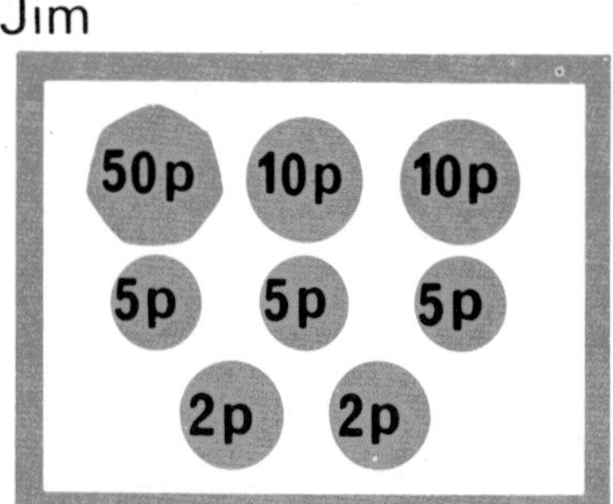

Jack

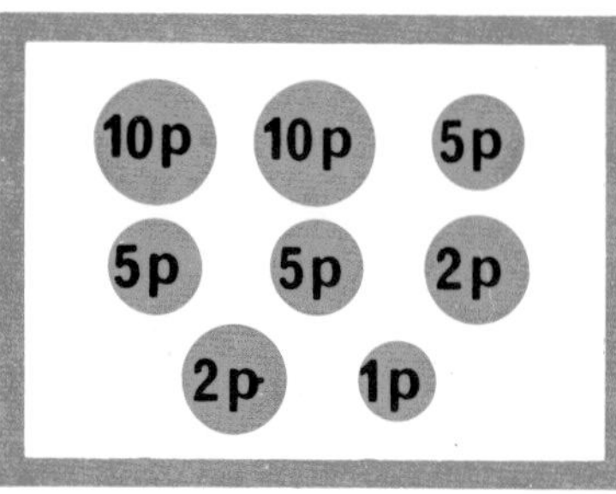

Bob

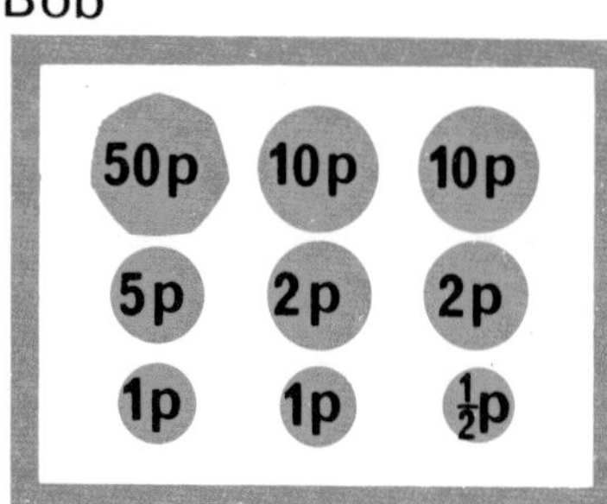

(**a**) How much money has each boy?
(**b**) Who has the most?
(**c**) Who has the least?
(**d**) How much has Bob more than Jack?
(**e**) How much more does Jack need to have the same as Jim?

We could use these coins to buy the knife:

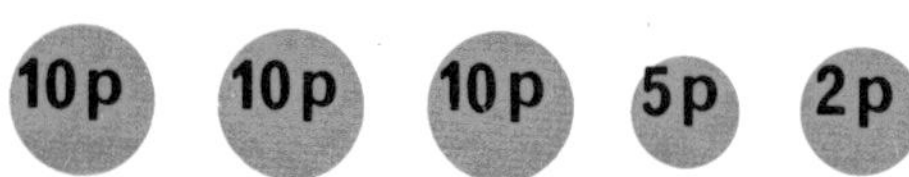

B Show how you could buy the things below. The number of coins is shown, but the names of some of them have been left out.
Copy the coins and put in the names which have been left out.

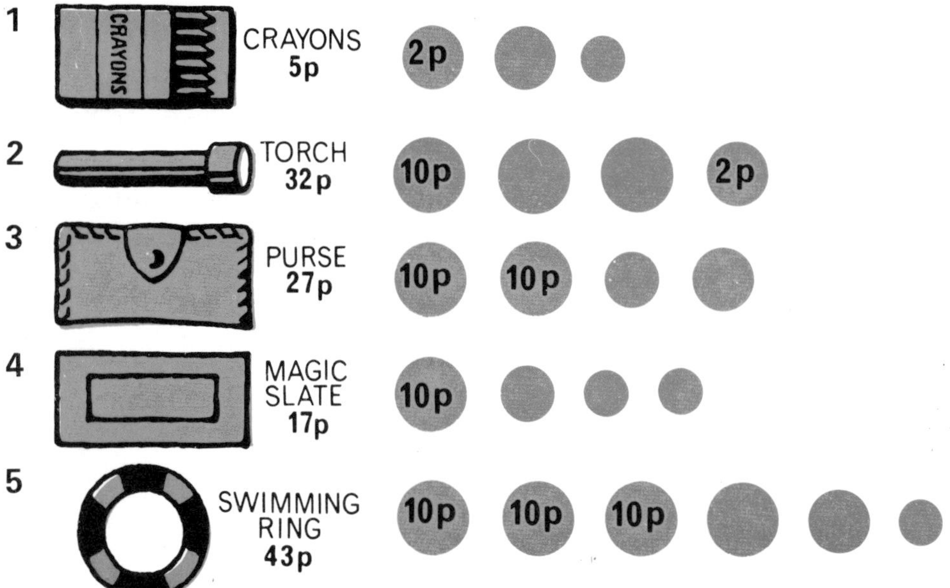

SUPERMARKET

Corned Beef	18p
Spam	23p
Ham and Pork	28p
Steak	19p
Corn Flakes	$12\frac{1}{2}$p
Rice Crispies	11p
Wonder Crisps	10p
Honey	26p
Jam	16p
Pears	15p
Plums	12p
Fruit Salad	11p
Garden Peas	5p
Pickles	12p
Salmon	24p
Coffee	46p

Here is what 6 women bought.
How much did each woman spend?

Mrs. Jeff: RICE CRISPIES, JAM, CORNED BEEF

Mrs. Dunn: CORN FLAKES, SALMON, HONEY

Mrs. Fry: WONDER CRISPS, PLUMS, SPAM

Mrs. Bull: STEAK, PEARS, HONEY, PEAS

Mrs. Will: RICE CRISPIES, CORN FLAKES, HAM PORK, FRUIT SALAD

Mrs. Jack: SALMON, COFFEE, PEARS, PICKLES

(**a**) How much had Mrs. Jeff left from a FIFTY?
(**b**) How much had Mrs. Bull left from a FIFTY and two TENS?

D **How a shopkeeper gives change**

If you buy a toy which costs 38p, and give the shopkeeper a 50p coin, he does this. He gives you the toy you bought and says, "38p and 2p make 40p, and 10p more makes 50p".

50p = 38p + 2p + 10p

This means he gives you 2p + 10p, or 12p in change.
Instead of subtracting he adds to make up the amount you gave him.

Show how a shopkeeper would give change.
You may use real or "pretend" money to help you.

	YOU BUY	GIVE THE SHOPKEEPER
1	A box of Smarties at $7\frac{1}{2}$p	**10p**
2	A stick of rock at 20p	**50p**
3	A cake at 8p	**10p**
4	A small cake at 3p	**5p**
5	A toy at 12p	**10p + 10p**
6	A Mars bar at $4\frac{1}{2}$p	**10p**
7	A pen at 7p	**5p + 5p**
8	A toy car at 17p	**10p + 5p + 5p**
9	Fruit at 18p	**50p**
10	A box of chocolates at 16p	**10p + 5p + 2p**

E

1

Make these amounts up to 10p	
2p	**$4\frac{1}{2}$p**
5p	**$7\frac{1}{2}$p**
7p	**$8\frac{1}{2}$p**
8p	**$3\frac{1}{2}$p**
9p	**$1\frac{1}{2}$p**

2

Make these amounts up to 20p	
9p	**3p**
5p	**4p**
8p	**10p**
15p	**$12\frac{1}{2}$p**
12p	**$16\frac{1}{2}$p**

3

Make these amounts up to 50p	
30p	**42p**
20p	**32p**
10p	**$46\frac{1}{2}$p**
12p	**$40\frac{1}{2}$p**
38p	**$25\frac{1}{2}$p**

If you like, use real money or "pretend" money to help you.

F Pounds and New Pence

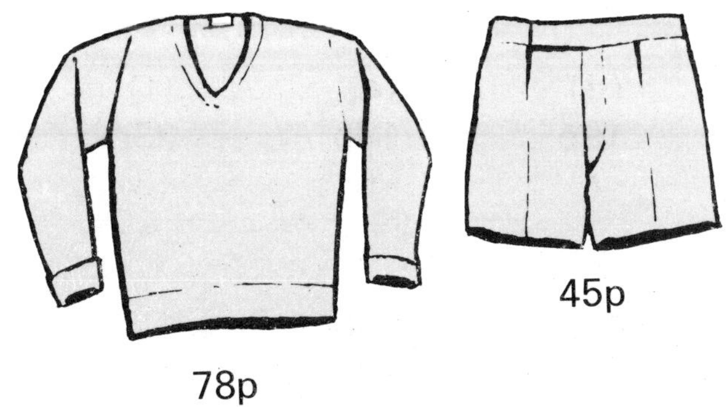

Dad bought me a pullover and a pair of shorts.
How much did they cost him?
They cost 78p + 45p = 123p.
When the new pence amount to more than 100p we usually change them to pounds.

100 new pence = £1

So 123p = £1 and 23p.
A short way of writing this is £1·23.
Note that instead of the word "and" we use a point.
Note also we miss out the "p" sign.
We never use the £ sign and the "p" sign together.
The point separates the pounds and the new pence.

124p = £1·24
176p = £1·76
185p = £1·85

1 Write in this way:

130p	118p	139p	147p
152p	125p	143p	162p

£1·25 = 125p
£1·70 = 170p
£1·02 = 102p

2 Write in this way:

£1·24	£1·12	£1·36	£1·48
£1·95	£1·05	£1·08	£1·03

G We can read £1·24 in two ways:

1 One pound and 24 new pence.
2 One pound twenty-four.

Read these in two ways:

£1·15 £1·50 £1·35 £1·76 £2·20 £3·84

Write these using the £ sign and the "point":

(**a**) One pound twenty (**b**) One pound sixteen
(**c**) One pound ten (**d**) One pound forty-five
(**e**) Two pounds sixty (**f**) Two pounds twelve

Note carefully: When writing pounds and new pence together there are always two figures after the "point".

We must be careful when the number of new pence is less than 10.
One pound nine is written £1·09, never £1·9. (What does £1·90 mean?)
In the same way one pound five is £1·05.

H Write in this way:

(**a**) One pound seven (**b**) One pound six
(**c**) One pound two (**d**) Two pounds three
(**e**) Two pounds eight (**f**) Two pounds one

I Multiplying money

We multiply the number of new pence in the usual way. We put "p" in the answer to show that the answer is new pence.

Do these. The first two are done for you:

	(a)	(b)	(c)	(d)	(e)	(f)
1	36p	15p	16p	19p	18p	23p
	×2	×5	×3	×4	×5	×3
	72p	75p				
2	48p	24p	23p	47p	19p	17p
	×2	×3	×4	×2	×3	×5
3	37p	32p	19p	24p	45p	25p
	×2	×3	×5	×4	×2	×4

4 Find the cost of:

(a) 3 tins of pears at 15p each.
(b) 5 tins of garden peas at 7p each.
(c) 4 jars of jam at 15p each.
(d) 2 tins of soup at $9\frac{1}{2}$p each.

5 Find the cost of:

(a) 3 jars of honey at 26p each.
(b) 4 tins of plums at 13p each.
(c) 2 packets of corn flakes at $12\frac{1}{2}$p each.
(d) 5 jars of jam at 17p each.

J Dividing money

We divide in the usual way. We always put the "p" sign in the answer to show that the answer is money.

Now do these. The first one is done for you:

	(a)	(b)	(c)	(d)	(e)	(f)
	15p					
1	3)45p	2)90p	2)36p	3)75p	4)52p	5)90p
2	2)76p	3)72p	4)72p	5)75p	4)76p	3)84p
3	3)45p	4)68p	5)65p	2)92p	5)95p	4)96p

4 **(a)** 3 tins of fruit cost 42p. Find the cost of 1 tin.
(b) 4 tubes of Smarties cost 28p. Find the cost of 1 tube.
(c) 5 tins of toffee cost 85p. Find the cost of 1 tin.

5 **(a)** 2 balls cost 78p. Find the price of each ball.
(b) 3 ball point pens cost 39p. What does 1 pen cost?
(c) 4 rulers cost 56p. How much does each ruler cost?

Parts of wholes

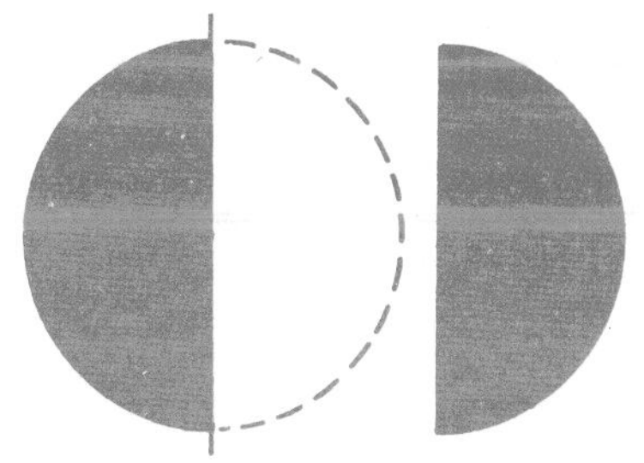

A If your mother gave you an orange and told you to give your little brother a half of it, you would know what to do, wouldn't you? You would cut it or break it into two parts of the same size and give him one of these parts.

A half is usually written as $\frac{1}{2}$ (1 part out of 2 equal parts). You already know this because you always write a half penny as $\frac{1}{2}$p.

You can see then that to find a half of anything, you just divide it by 2.

1 Dick had 14 marbles. He gave Tom a half of them. How many did Tom get?

2 Jean had 20 beads. She lost half of them. How many did she lose?

3 Mother bought a dozen eggs. She used half of them for baking. How many eggs had she left?

4 Fred found 16 conkers. He gave Jim half of them. How many conkers did Jim get?

5 Mary bought 8 caramels. She ate half of them. How many did she eat?

6 Teacher had 18 chalks in a box. When she had used half of them, how many had she left?

B

Jack bought a bar of cream chocolate. It was divided into 4 equal parts. Each part is called a **quarter** of the whole.
1 quarter is written as $\frac{1}{4}$ (1 part out of 4 equal parts). You can see that to find a quarter of anything we just divide it by 4.
So $\frac{1}{4}$ of 8 cakes $=$ 2 cakes.

1 Jim had 12 marbles. He gave Bill $\frac{1}{4}$ of them. How many did Bill get?

2 Harry had 8 sweets. He ate $\frac{1}{4}$ of them. How many sweets did he eat?

3 Kate had 20 pennies. She spent $\frac{1}{4}$ of them. How many pennies did she spend?

4 Mr Jones had 16 golf balls. While playing a game he lost $\frac{1}{4}$ of them. How many did he lose?

5 Mother bought 24 plums. She gave me $\frac{1}{4}$ of them. How many did I get?

6 There are 28 boys in my class. $\frac{1}{4}$ of them have curly hair. How many curly haired boys are there in the class?

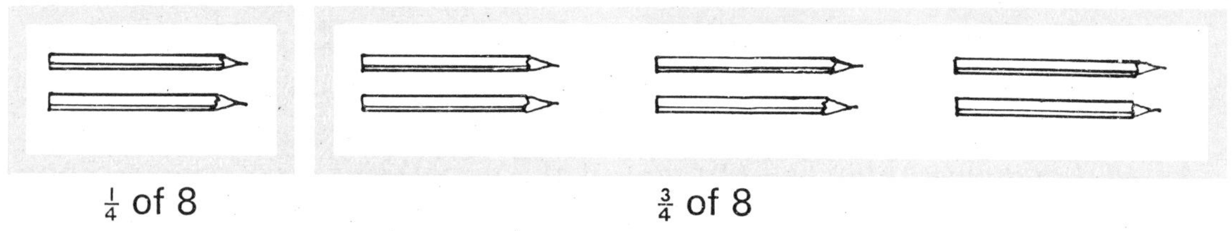

$\frac{1}{4}$ of 8 $\frac{3}{4}$ of 8

Take 8 pencils, or straws, or books and put them in twos on your desk as you see here.

Each two is $\frac{1}{4}$ of 8. You can see that $\frac{3}{4}$ of 8 $= 6$

$\frac{1}{4}$ of 8 $= 2$ $\frac{3}{4}$ of 8 $= 6$ So $\frac{3}{4}$ is 3 times $\frac{1}{4}$.

Let's try this in another way with a larger number.
Here is a line divided into 16 equal parts.

$\frac{1}{4}$ of 16

$\frac{3}{4}$ of 16

You can see that $\frac{3}{4}$ of 16 $= 12$ and $\frac{1}{4}$ of 16 $= 4$

So once again you can see that $\frac{3}{4} = 3$ times $\frac{1}{4}$

Don't you see now that we have found an easy way to find $\frac{3}{4}$ of any number? All we need to do is to find $\frac{1}{4}$ and then multiply by 3. Suppose we want to find $\frac{3}{4}$ of 20.

$\frac{1}{4}$ of 20 $= 5$ $\frac{3}{4}$ of 20 $= 5 \times 3 = 15$.

Find in this way:

$\frac{3}{4}$ of 24 $\frac{3}{4}$ of 32 $\frac{3}{4}$ of 36 $\frac{3}{4}$ of 40 $\frac{3}{4}$ of 48.

1 John had 12 marbles. He lost $\frac{3}{4}$ of them in a game. How many did he lose?

2 Mabel had 16 sweets. She ate $\frac{3}{4}$ of them. How many did she eat?

3 Edna got 100 pennies from Daddy on her birthday. She spent $\frac{3}{4}$ of them. How many did she spend?

4 Harry planted 80 leeks in his garden. His mother used $\frac{3}{4}$ of them. How many did she use?

5 There were 56 cars in a car park. $\frac{3}{4}$ of them were small cars. How many small cars were there?

6 A fisherman caught 88 fish. He gave $\frac{3}{4}$ of them to his friends. How many did he give away?

Decimals

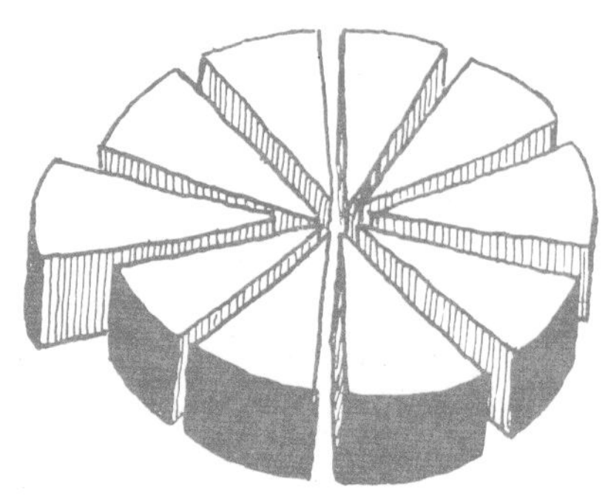

A Above is a whole cake cut into a number of equal sized pieces.
How many pieces?

Here is one of these equal pieces—one piece out of 10 equal pieces.
And we know that "one piece out of 10 equal pieces" is written $\frac{1}{10}$ (1 tenth).

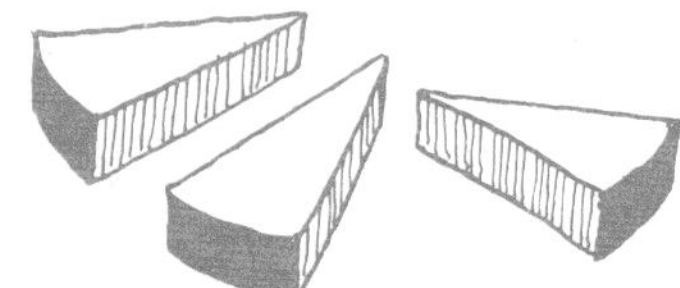

Here are 3 pieces out of 10 equal pieces.
Write this as a fraction of the whole cake.

We divide things so often into tenths that we may write tenths in a short way, like this:

$\frac{1}{10} = \cdot 1$ (we read this as **"point one"**)

$\frac{3}{10} = \cdot 3$ (we read this as **"point three"**)

Write this table in your excercise book and finish it.

1 tenth $= \frac{1}{10} = \cdot 1$
2 tenths $= \frac{2}{10} = \cdot 2$
3 tenths $=$
⋮
9 tenths $=$

Fractions like ·1, ·2, ·3 are called decimals.
Remember
the figure after the "point" always stands for tenths.

B

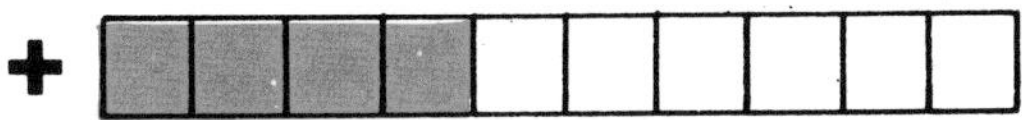

Here we have 2 strips of cardboard of the same size.
The second strip is divided into tenths.
The whole strip and $\frac{4}{10}$ (4 tenths) of the second strip are coloured.

So 1 whole $+\frac{4}{10}$ of a whole is coloured.

1 whole $+\frac{4}{10}$ of a whole can be written as 1 whole $+$ ·4 of a whole.

A shorter way of writing 1 whole $+$ ·4 of a whole is 1·4.

2 wholes $+\frac{5}{10}$ of a whole is 2·5.

1 Write these in the decimal way:

(a) 1 whole $+\frac{7}{10}$ of a whole
(b) 2 wholes $+\frac{1}{10}$ of a whole
(c) 3 wholes $+\frac{9}{10}$ of a whole
(d) 4 wholes $+\frac{8}{10}$ of a whole
(e) 7 wholes $+\frac{6}{10}$ of a whole
(f) 9 wholes $+\frac{4}{10}$ of a whole

Remember the figure in front of the **point** stands for **wholes**
The figure after the **point** stands for **tenths.**

We read 1·3 as "one point three" and 4·5 as "four point five".

2 Write what these mean:

(a) 1·2 (b) 2·7 (c) 3·9 (d) 6·8 (e) 9·1 (f) 10·4

3 Write in the decimal way:

(a) $1\frac{3}{10}$ (b) $4\frac{1}{10}$ (c) $6\frac{7}{10}$ (d) $5\frac{2}{10}$ (e) $8\frac{9}{10}$ (f) $10\frac{5}{10}$

4 Here are four picture numbers. Write the numbers in figures. Use the decimal point to separate the whole numbers from the tenths.

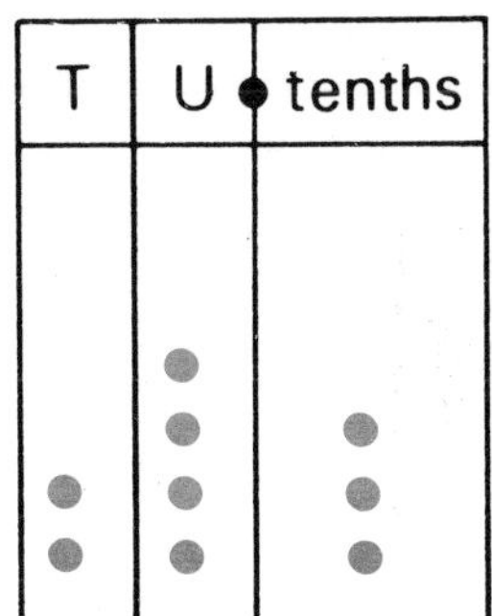

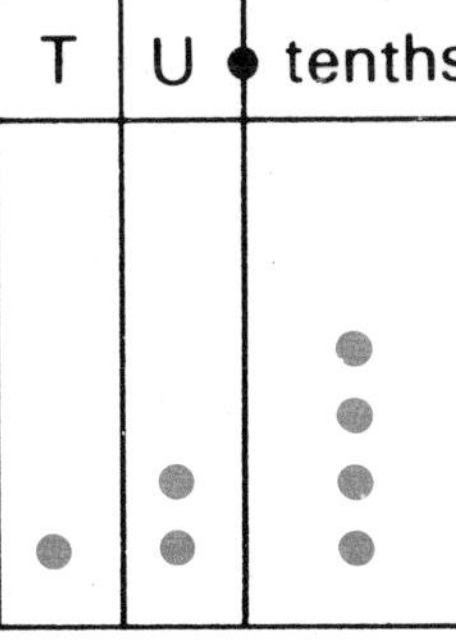

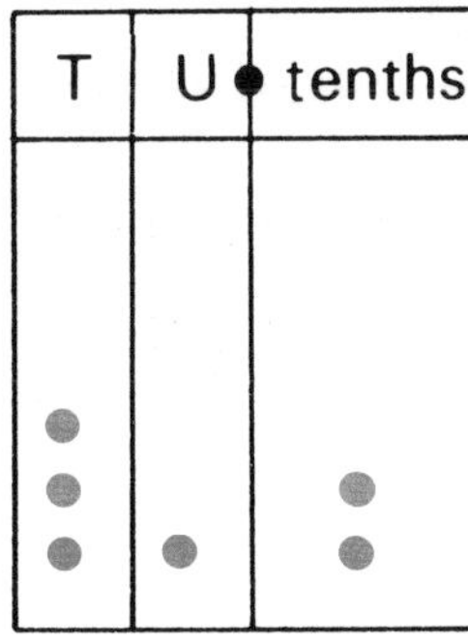

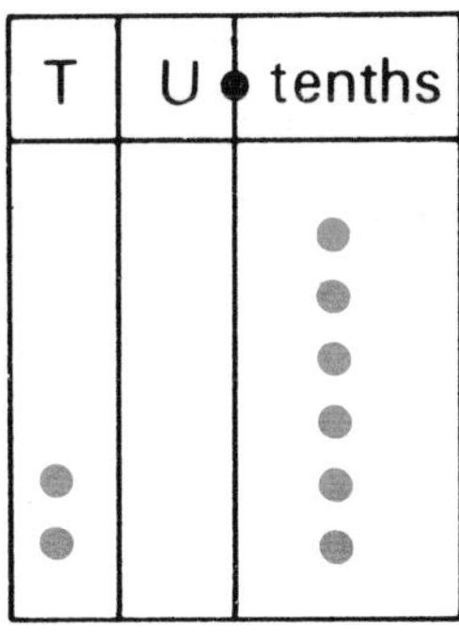

Draw picture numbers of your own to show these numbers:

(a) 15·2 (b) 21·4 (c) 34·7 (d) 11·5 (e) 30·8

Squares and rectangles

This shape is called a **Square**.
How many sides has it?
How many corners has it?
Measure the length of each side.
What do you find?
Test the corners with your right angle measure.
What do you find?

Get a coloured paper square. Fold it as shown in the first drawing (1) and you will get a different shape.
Measure the sides of the new shape. What do you find?
How many sides has it?
How many corners has it?
Test the corners. What do you find?
Is this new shape a square?
This new shape is called a **Rectangle**.
You can see that two of the sides are longer than the other two sides.

Fold

(1)

Is this page a square or a rectangle?
Fold the new shape as in drawing (2).
What is the shape now?
Now open up your folded paper.

Fold

(2)

How many shapes do the creases make and what shape are they?
There are plenty of things in your classroom with a rectangle shape.
See how many you can find.

B

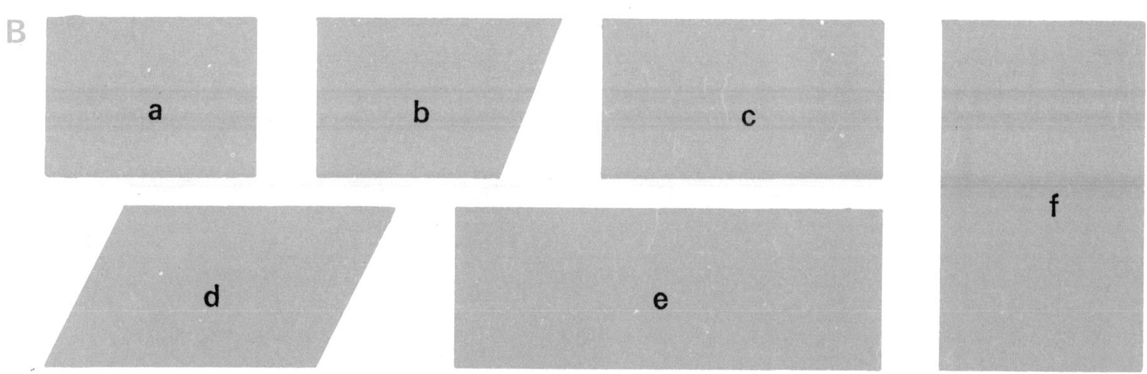

Which of these shapes are rectangles?
(Remember that a rectangle has 4 square corners.)

C

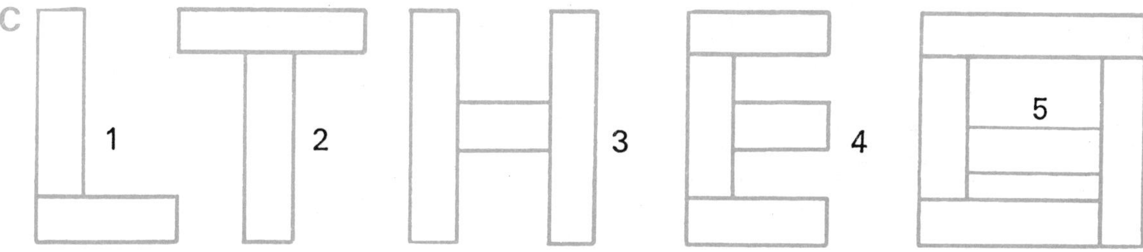

How many rectangles are there in each of these shapes?

D

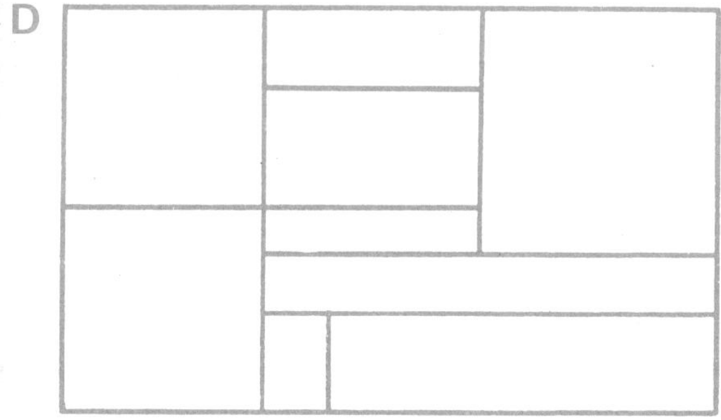

How many squares can you see in the drawing?
How do you know they are squares?
How many rectangles can you see in the drawing?
How do you know they are rectangles?

E Make some squares and some rectangles on your nail-board with elastic bands. You can see that squares always have the same shape, but they can be any size. You can have large squares and small squares. Every square has four sides the same length, and four square corners.
Every rectangle has four square corners, but two of the sides are always longer than the other two sides.

Table of threes

A

1 Make these three patterns with counters or on your peg board and then copy them into your exercise book.

Under the right pattern write:

3 ones $= 3$	3 twos $= 6$	3 threes $= 9$
$1 \times 3 = 3$	$2 \times 3 = 6$	$3 \times 3 = 9$
$3 \times 1 = 3$	$3 \times 2 = 6$	$9 \div 3 = 3$
$3 \div 3 = 1$	$6 \div 3 = 2$	
$3 \div 1 = 3$	$6 \div 2 = 3$	

B **2** Now make the patterns of 3 fours, 3 fives, 3 sixes, and so on up to 3 tens. Under each pattern write the multiplication and division facts you discover. Write the Table of Threes in your Multiplication Square

If "**c**" stands for the missing figure, find what "**c**" is.

1	$c = 4 \times 3$	**9**	$c = 30 \div 3$
2	$c = 6 \times 3$	**10**	$c = 21 \div 3$
3	$c = 9 \times 3$	**11**	$27 \div 3 = c$
4	$c = 8 \times 3$	**12**	$15 \div 3 = c$
5	$c = 7 \times 3$	**13**	$9 \div 3 = c$
6	$c = 12 \div 3$	**14**	$3 \times c = 9$
7	$c = 18 \div 3$	**15**	$10 \times 3 = c$
8	$c = 24 \div 3$	**16**	$15 \div 3 = c$

C Do these in your exercise book:

	(a)	(b)	(c)	(d)
1	13×3	16×3	23×3	32×3
2	25×3	30×3	26×3	19×3
3	38×3	47×3	29×3	56×3
4	62×3	65×3	73×3	84×3

D Do these in your exercise book:

	(a)	(b)	(c)	(d)
1	$3\overline{)21}$	$3\overline{)30}$	$3\overline{)15}$	$3\overline{)27}$
2	$3\overline{)39}$	$3\overline{)36}$	$3\overline{)45}$	$3\overline{)47}$
3	$3\overline{)42}$	$3\overline{)48}$	$3\overline{)54}$	$3\overline{)60}$
4	$3\overline{)32}$	$3\overline{)38}$	$3\overline{)22}$	$3\overline{)69}$
5	$3\overline{)67}$	$3\overline{)91}$	$3\overline{)95}$	$3\overline{)99}$
6	$3\overline{)75}$	$3\overline{)77}$	$3\overline{)81}$	$3\overline{)88}$

E **1** There are 3 rows of boys in the playground. There are 19 boys in each row. How many boys is this altogether?

2 Share 24 sweets equally among 3 boys. How many will each get?

3 Three rows of books. 23 books in each row. How many books altogether?

4 How often can I take 3 pencils from a box holding 36 pencils?

5 A milk crate holds 24 bottles. How many bottles can 3 crates hold?

6 Four of these numbers do not divide evenly by three. Pick them out.

12, 18, 25, 30, 44, 27, 29, 62.

7 If $y = 30 \div 3$, what does y stand for?

8 What number does y stand for if $y = (10 \times 3) + 6$?

9 There are three rows of cars in a car park. There are 20 cars in each row. How many cars are there in the car park?

10 Three boys gathered 12 conkers and another boy gathered 6 conkers. How many conkers altogether did the boys gather?

11 I gave Tom 29 sweets and told him to share them equally among his three chums and to keep what was left over to himself.

(a) How many did Tom give to each chum?

(b) How many did he himself get?

12 If $\mathbf{n} = (27 \div 3) + 4$, what number does **n** stand for?

13 Four of these numbers when divided by 3 have a remainder of 2. Pick out these four numbers:

14, 16, 19, 20, 23, 27, 32.

Table of sixes

A

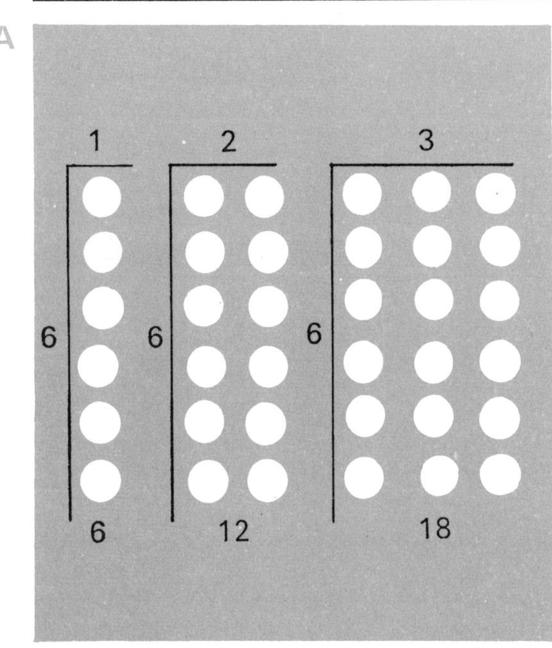

1 Make these patterns and then copy them into your exercise book. Under each pattern write all the multiplication and division facts you discover. Learn these facts.

2 Make the patterns of 6 fours, 6 fives, and so on up to 6 tens. Under each pattern write all the multiplication and division facts you discover. Learn these facts.

3 Now write the Table of Sixes in your Multiplication Square.

4 How could you use the Table of Threes in your square to fill in the Table of Sixes ?

B If the letter b stands for the missing number, find what b is.

1	$b = 3 \times 6$	4	$b = 8 \times 6$	**7**	$24 \div 6 = b$	**10**	$60 \div 6 = b$
2	$b = 5 \times 6$	**5**	$b = 9 \times 6$	**8**	$30 \div 6 = b$	**11**	$16 \div b = 2$
3	$b = 7 \times 6$	**6**	$b = 6 \times 6$	**9**	$42 \div 6 = b$	**12**	$54 \div b = 9$

C Multiply :

	(a)	(b)	(c)	(d)		(a)	(b)	(c)	(d)
1	11	12	15	17	**2**	16	20	23	28
	× 6	× 6	× 6	× 6		× 6	× 6	× 6	× 6

D Divide:

1 $6\overline{)32}$ $6\overline{)36}$ $6\overline{)27}$ $6\overline{)40}$

2 $6\overline{)54}$ $6\overline{)60}$ $6\overline{)72}$ $6\overline{)84}$

3 $6\overline{)25}$ $6\overline{)42}$ $6\overline{)45}$ $6\overline{)57}$

4 $6\overline{)90}$ $6\overline{)96}$ $6\overline{)75}$ $6\overline{)88}$

E **1** There are 48 eggs in a box. How many times can I take 6 eggs from it?

2 A bus can carry 38 people. How many people can 6 such buses carry?

3 There are 6 rows of cars in a car park. There are 24 cars in each row. How many cars are in the car park?

4 There are 72 caramels in a box. How many girls could get 6 each?

5 A man earns £18 in a week. How many pounds does he earn in 6 weeks?

6 John had 35 marbles. To how many boys could he give 6 each and how many would he have left?

7 Bill gave 10 marbles to each of his six chums and had 4 marbles left. How many marbles had he to start with?

8 There are 30 nuts in a bag. How many nuts are there in 6 bags?

9 There are 20 metres in a roll of cloth. How many metres are there in 6 rolls of the same size?

10 96 pennies were divided equally among 6 boys. How many did each boy get?

F **1** What number does **y** stand for if **y** $= (5 \times 6) + 4$?

2 Only three of these numbers divide evenly by 6. Pick them out.

18 26 32 38 42 24

3 How many groups of 6 are there in 54?

4 If $n = (60 \div 6) + 8$, what number does **n** stand for?

5 What are the next three numbers in this series?

6, 12, 18, 24, ?, ?, ?

6 How many eggs are there altogether in 6 boxes if there are 24 eggs in each box?

7 What number am I thinking of, if, when I multiply it by 6, I get 48?

8 What is the answer when you multiply 9 by 6 and then take away 4?

9 Divide 60 by 6 and then add 7.

10 **c** $= (7 \times 6) + (3 \times 6)$. Find the number that **c** stands for.

Measuring liquids

A Get a bowl, a jam jar, a milk bottle, a cup and other things that can hold water. We call these things **containers.** A funnel will help you to pour water into a container without spilling it.

1 Fill the cup with water and pour it into the bowl. Does it fill the bowl? See how many cupfuls the bowl holds.

2 Which can hold most water:

(a) an egg cup or a tea cup
(b) a tea cup or a basin
(c) a tea spoon or a saucer
(d) a medicine bottle or a spoon
(e) a tumbler or a pail
(f) a jug or a barrel?

3 Get a tea spoon and a medicine bottle. See how many spoonfuls the medicine bottle can hold. Use a funnel.

Tommy's Billy's

4 Tommy and Billy each brought a cup to school to measure how much some containers could hold. Tommy found that it took 3 cupfuls of his cup to fill a bowl. Do you think it took the same number of cupfuls of Billy's cup to fill the bowl?

Sue's Eva's

5 This picture shows Sue's and Eva's cups. Sue found it took 4 cupfuls to fill the bowl. How many cupfuls of Eva's cup do you think it took. Why?

B If all the cups in the world were the same size, like Sue's and Eva's, people everywhere could use cups to say how much liquid a container could hold. But all cups are not the same size, so we must use something that is the same everywhere.

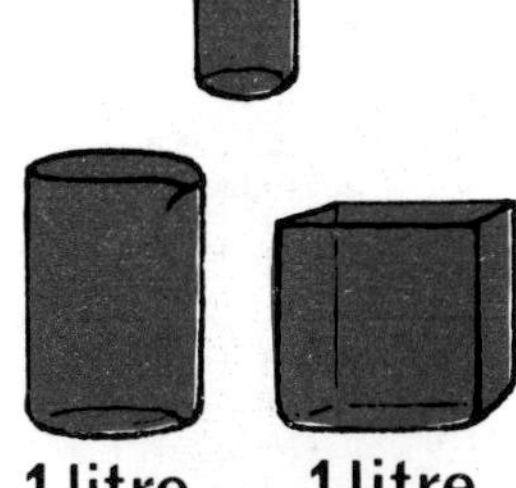

The measure we use is called a LITRE.

Your teacher will have a LITRE measure and also a HALF-LITRE measure.

There are different shapes of litre measures but they can all hold, when full, a litre of water, or milk or Coca-Cola.

Your litre measure may have a mark on it to show $\frac{1}{2}$ litre.

The short way of writing **litre** is **ℓ**.

1 Fill a school milk bottle with water and pour it into a litre measure.

Does it fill the litre measure?

Now see if it fills a half-litre measure?

2 See how many school milk bottles you can fill from a litre of water.

3 See if a cupful of water is more or less than a half litre.

4 Get some other bottles, some small and some big.

(a) Guess if the small bottles can hold more or less than $\frac{1}{2}$ litre of water. Now use your litre measure or your $\frac{1}{2}$ litre measure to find out if your guess was a good one.

(b) Guess if the larger bottles can hold more or less than 1 litre. Now measure with your litre measure.

(c) Try this with bottles of different sizes and shapes until they become quite good at guessing if they hold about $\frac{1}{2}$ litre, about 1 litre, or more than 1 litre.

1 Get some larger containers, like a bowl, a pail, a basin and a watering can.
Pour a litre of water into each of them, in turn, and then try to guess how many litres each can hold.
Now pour more water into each container until it is full.
About how many litres did each hold?
Did you guess well?

2 How many times can the can be filled from the drum of oil?

3 (**a**) How many bottles of this size can be filled from the cask of wine?
(**b**) How many litres of wine would be left in the cask?

Measuring weight

A You will need things like books, beanbags, stones, nails, tins, sand, peas, beads and marbles. You will also need scales and weights.

1 Take a book in one hand and a stone in the other.
Which do you think is the heavier?
Which does your neighbour think is the heavier?
2 Do the same with other things and say which you think is the heavier.

B It is easy to find out which of two things is the heavier by using scales.

1 Put your stone in one pan and your book in the other pan. Which is the heavier?
Were you right when you tried to guess?
2 Do the same with the other things you tried in your hands.
3 Put a stone in one pan and sand in the other pan until the two sides balance. Now do the same thing with a book in one pan.
4 Try this with nails in one pan and marbles or pebbles in the other pan.

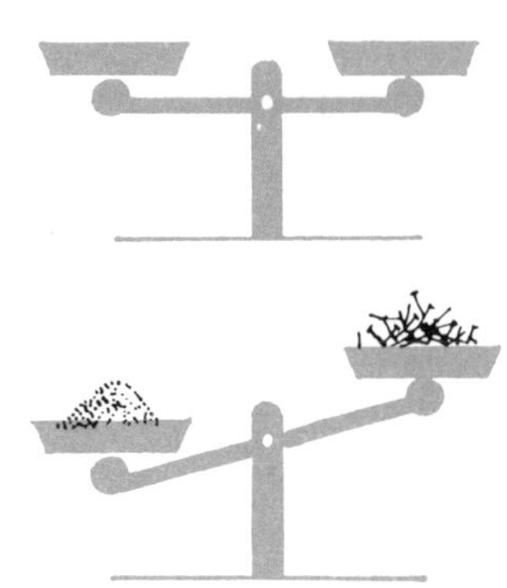

Kilogramme

C When you go to a butcher's shop to buy meat, the butcher does not just guess the weight of the meat you want. He puts weights on one side of his scales and then he adds meat to the other side until both sides balance.
The most important weight is the **1 KILOGRAMME** weight.

The short way of writing **kilogramme** is **kg**.
A **kilogramme** is often called a **kilo**.
Mum may buy **1 kg** of sugar or **2 kg** of potatoes.
She would ask for a **kilo** of sugar or 2 **kilos** of potatoes.

1 Take a kilogramme weight in one hand. Now take up some things like a school bag full of books, a beanbag, a brick, in your other hand and find out which you think weighs more than, or less than, 1 kg.
Your arms will be like a pair of scales.
Now use your scales to see if you were right.

2 Look around for something you think weighs about a kilogramme. Now put it on the scales to see if you were right.

3 Fill a bag with sand to balance the **1 kg** weight. You can use this bag as your own kilogramme weight and use it on your scales.

Another weight which is often used is a half kilogramme. It is marked $\frac{1}{2}$ **kg**.
It is often called a **half-kilo**.

4 See if you can find some things you think would weigh about $\frac{1}{2}$ kg and then use your scales to see if you were right.

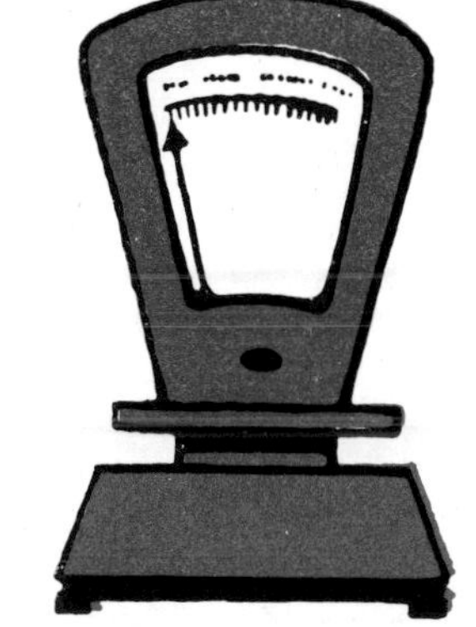

Shops use different kinds of scales.
Some use scales with weights. Others use scales with a pointer which points to the weight of the thing being weighed.
When you are in a shop look to see the kind of scales used.

Grammes

D Things that do not weigh nearly as much as a kilogramme are weighed in **GRAMMES**.
A **gramme** is a very small weight, not much heavier than a bee.
It is so small that it takes 1 000 grammes to make 1 kilogramme.

1 KILOGRAMME = 1000 GRAMMES
$\frac{1}{2}$ KILOGRAMME = 500 GRAMMES

For short we write grammes as **g**.
So 75 grammes is written 75 g.
Write in this short way:
80 grammes   120 grammes   245 grammes   364 grammes
What do these mean:
100 g   96 g   234 g   382 g   450 g?

Copy and fill in the missing numbers of grammes.

1 300g = 200g + ☐
2 400g = 200g + ☐
3 200g = 100g + 50g + ☐
4 $\frac{1}{2}$kg = 300g + ☐
5 $\frac{1}{2}$kg = 200g + 200g + ☐
6 1kg = 900g + ☐
7 1kg = 800g + 100g + ☐
8 1kg = 600g + 200g + ☐

Here are some things seen in a supermarket.
The weight of the contents of each tin or packet is marked in grammes (g).

(**a**) Which of these articles weigh more than $\frac{1}{2}$ kg (500 g)?

(**b**) Which weigh less than $\frac{1}{2}$ kg?

(**c**) Which is the heaviest?

(**d**) Which weighs least?

(**e**) How many grammes more than $\frac{1}{2}$ kg does the bag of flour weigh?

(**f**) How many grammes less than $\frac{1}{2}$ kg does the tin of carrots weigh?

(**g**) Make a list of these articles with their weights. Write them in order, beginning with the article that weighs most.

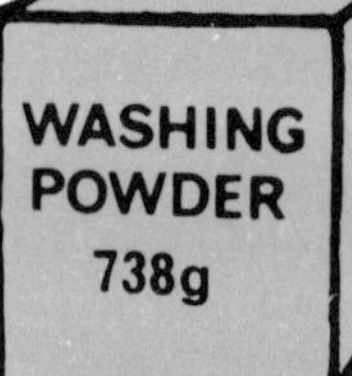

Bring to school as many packets and tins as you can, showing the number of grammes that the contents weigh.
Empty packets and tins will do.
Now from the packets and tins brought by the class make up a list, like this:

Less than $\frac{1}{2}$ kg (500 g)	More than $\frac{1}{2}$ kg (500 g)
Margarine 228 g	Sugar 907 g

Table of nines

You should now be able to fill in the Table of Nines in your Multiplication Square. You could use the Table of Threes in your square to help you. How?

Now write the Table of Nines up to 9 times 10 in this way:—

$1 \times 9 = 9$	$9 \times 1 = 9$	$9 \div 9 = 1$
$2 \times 9 = 18$	$9 \times 2 = 18$	$18 \div 9 = 2$
$3 \times 9 = 27$	$9 \times 3 = 27$	$27 \div 9 = 3$
$4 \times 9 = 36$	$9 \times 4 = 36$	$36 \div 9 = 4$

A If y stands for the missing number, find what y is.

1	$y = 3 \times 9$	**5**	$y = 4 \times 9$	**9**	$y = 18 \div 9$	**13**	$54 \div 9 = y$
2	$y = 5 \times 9$	**6**	$3 \times 9 = y$	**10**	$y = 36 \div 9$	**14**	$90 \div 9 = y$
3	$y = 7 \times 9$	**7**	$10 \times 9 = y$	**11**	$y = 27 \div 9$	**15**	$72 \div 9 = y$
4	$y = 6 \times 9$	**8**	$9 \times 9 = y$	**12**	$y = 45 \div 9$	**16**	$63 \div 9 = y$

B Multiply

	(a)	(b)	(c)	(d)
1	11×9	12×9	14×9	17×9
2	18×9	20×9	23×9	24×9
3	25×9	21×9	32×9	36×9

C Divide

1	$9\overline{)36}$	$9\overline{)45}$	$9\overline{)27}$	$9\overline{)63}$
2	$9\overline{)19}$	$9\overline{)47}$	$9\overline{)38}$	$9\overline{)40}$
3	$9\overline{)21}$	$9\overline{)46}$	$9\overline{)90}$	$9\overline{)95}$
4	$9\overline{)49}$	$9\overline{)29}$	$9\overline{)13}$	$9\overline{)47}$
5	$9\overline{)75}$	$9\overline{)70}$	$9\overline{)54}$	$9\overline{)59}$
6	$9\overline{)92}$	$9\overline{)22}$	$9\overline{)82}$	$9\overline{)85}$

Telling the time

Look carefully at a clock face and you will see the hours marked round it. Between these numbers you will see small minute marks. There are 60 of these minute marks, because there are 60 minutes in 1 hour. The small hand on the clock tells us the hour o'clock (o'clock means "Of the clock".) The big hand points to the minutes.
Look at the first clock face. The small hand points to 3 and the big hand points straight up, so the time is 3 o'clock.

1 What is the time on each of the other clock faces?

You can see that the small hand has moved past 1. The big hand points to a quarter past, so the time is "a quarter past 1".

2 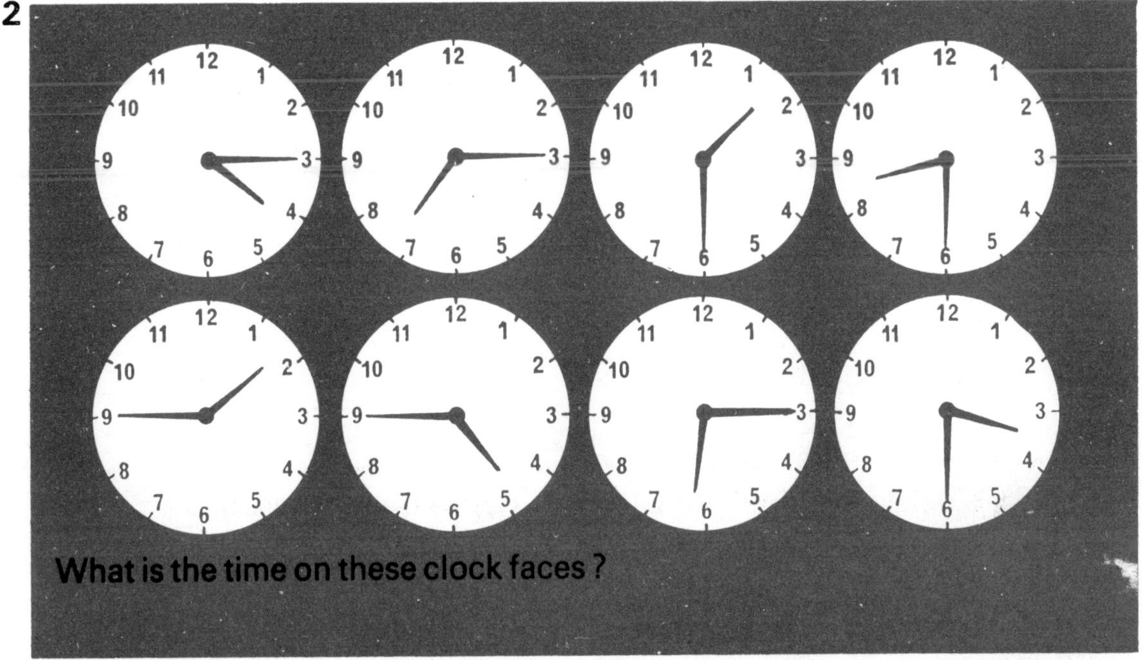

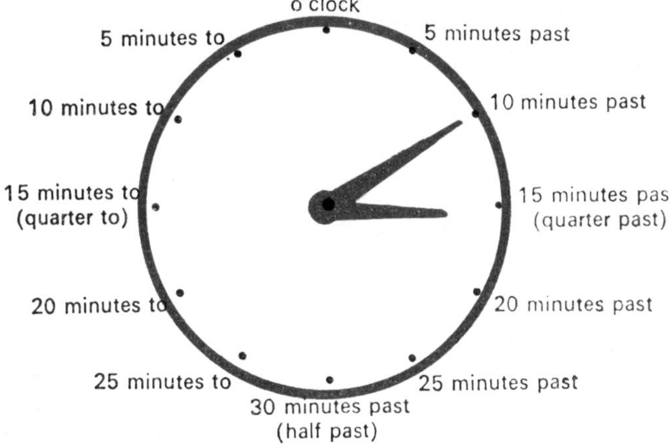

Learn to count quickly in fives up to 30:

5 — 10 — 15 — 20 — 25 — 30

You can see from the drawing above that as the big hand (the minute hand) moves on from 12 o'clock it shows minutes past o'clock until it passes 6. When it passes 6 it shows minutes to the next hour.
You can see that the time on the clock face above is 10 minutes past 3.

3

What is the time on these clock faces ?

4 How many minutes is it from :

(a) 3 o'clock to 10 minutes past 3.

(b) 5 minutes past 2 to a quarter past 2.

(c) 4 o'clock to a quarter past 4.

(d) 10 minutes past 8 to half past 8.

(e) 20 minutes past 3 to half past 3.

(f) Half past 2 to 10 minutes to 3.

(g) A quarter past 5 to a quarter to 6.

(h) Half past 6 to a quarter to 7.

(i) Half past 6 to 5 minutes to 7.

(j) 25 minutes past 8 to 25 minutes to 9 ?

5 A bus should have left at five minutes past 9. It was ten minutes late in leaving. At what time did it leave ?

6 School goes in at a quarter past nine. Kate was five minutes late. At what time did Kate come to school ?

7 A train should have arrived in Glasgow at twenty minutes to five. It was a quarter of an hour late. At what time did it arrive ?

8 I had to catch a train at half past eight. I arrived at the station five minutes early. At what time did I arrive ?

9 A football match started at a quarter past 3. I arrived ten minutes before it started. At what time did I arrive ?

10 I had to meet Ella at a quarter to seven to go to the pictures. She was five minutes late. At what time did she meet me ?

11 What time is it half an hour after a quarter past 4 ?

12 What time is it a quarter of an hour after 5 minutes to 6 ?

Fun with shapes

We are going to make up some pictures with squares, rectangles and triangles. You will need some coloured squares.

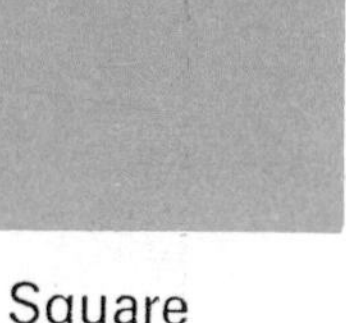

Square

Fold

Cut along fold

We can make some triangles from the squares.

Square

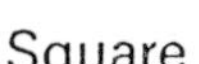

Fold

Cut along fold

We can make triangles from the rectangles by joining the corners with a pencil line and cutting along the line.

Make some small and some bigger squares and rectangles.
From these cut out some small and some bigger triangles.
Now let's make some pictures which you can paste into your exercise book.

Here are some pictures to help you.

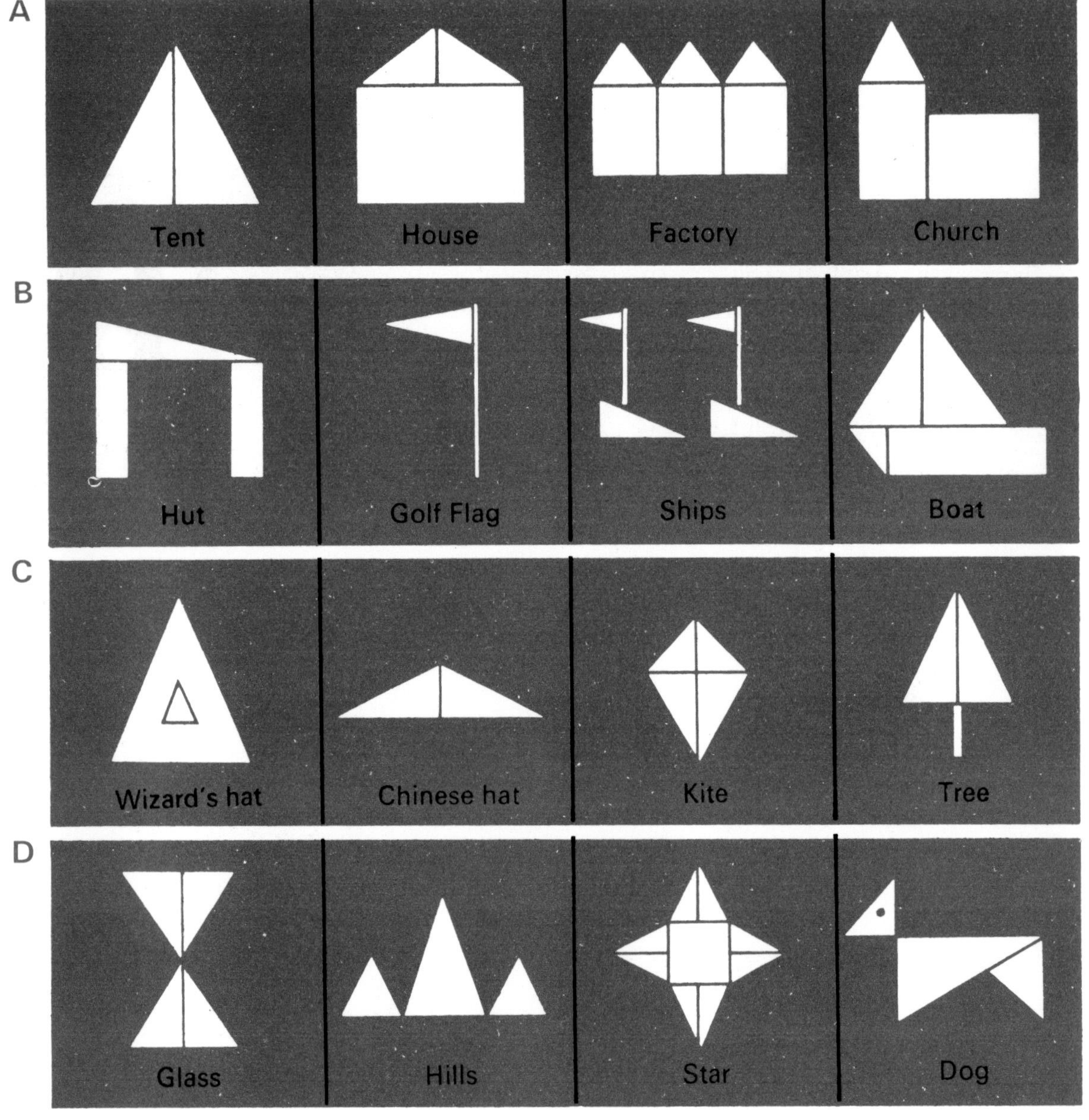

Now see how many pictures you can make up from these shapes.

Table of sevens

7 ones = 7
$1 \times 7 = 7$
$7 \times 1 = 7$
$7 \div 7 = 1$

7 twos = 14
$2 \times 7 = 14$
$7 \times 2 = 14$
$14 \div 7 = 2$
$14 \div 2 = 7$

7 threes = 21
$3 \times 7 = 21$
$7 \times 3 = 21$
$21 \div 7 = 3$
$21 \div 3 = 7$

1 Make these patterns in your exercise book and under each write the multiplication and division facts. Learn these facts.

2 Make the patterns of 7 fours, 7 fives, and so on up to 7 tens and under each pattern write all the multiplication and division facts you discover.

3 Now fill in the 7 Row and the 7 Column in your Multiplication Square.
Some of it has already been filled in.

Your multiplication square 2

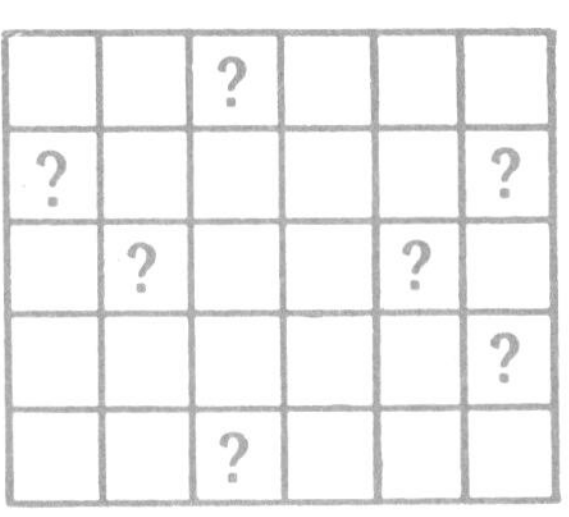

Here is the completed square up to the Table of Tens.

Check your own from this

Column

Row

×	**0**	**1**	**2**	**3**	**4**	**5**	**6**	**7**	**8**	**9**	**10**
0	0	0	0	0	0	0	0	0	0	0	0
1	0	1	2	3	4	5	6	7	8	9	10
2	0	2	4	6	8	10	12	14	16	18	20
3	0	3	6	9	12	15	18	21	24	27	30
4	0	4	8	12	16	20	24	28	32	36	40
5	0	5	10	15	20	25	30	35	40	45	50
6	0	6	12	18	24	30	36	42	48	54	60
7	0	7	14	21	28	35	42	49	56	63	70
8	0	8	16	24	32	40	48	56	64	72	80
9	0	9	18	27	36	45	54	63	72	81	90
10	0	10	20	30	40	50	60	70	80	90	100

A From your square fill in the next two numbers in these series of numbers:

1 2, 4, 6, 8, 10, — —

2 5, 10, 15, 20, 25, — —

3 3, 6, 9, 12, 15, — —

4 10, 20, 30, 40, 50, — —

5 21, 28, 35, 42 — —

6 24, 32, 40, 48 — —

7 30, 27, 24, 21 — —

8 1, 4, 9, 16, 25 — —

B Find what *'a'* and *'b'* stand for:

1 3, 6, a, 12, 15, b
2 a, 15, 20, b, 30, 35
3 20, 18, a, 14, b, 10
4 90, 80, 70, a, b, 40
5 20, 24, a, b, 36.
6 14, 21, 28, 35, a, b.
7 9, 18, a, 36, b, 54.
8 a, b, 56, 48, 40.

C Use your addition table and multiplication table to find the missing sign: (+ — × or ÷).

1 8 2 = 10
2 9 5 = 14
3 9 5 = 4
4 18 11 = 7
5 5 4 = 20
6 20 4 = 5
7 18 3 = 6
8 5 3 = 15
9 15 5 = 3
10 21 8 = 29
11 16 4 = 4
12 20 12 = 8
13 6 4 = 24
14 3 10 = 30
15 4 2 = 2

D Find the number y stands for:

1 $8 + y = 17$
2 $10 - y = 7$
3 $3 \times y = 18$
4 $5 \times y = 20$
5 $10 \div y = 2$
6 $14 + y = 20$
7 $14 - y = 5$
8 $y \times 4 = 24$
9 $y \div 3 = 7$
10 $y \div 5 = 30$
11 $23 + y = 40$
12 $y - 14 = 10$
13 $6 \times y = 48$
14 $32 \div y = 4$
15 $y + y = 10$

When figures are in brackets, work out each bracket separately, like this:

$$(4 \times 8) + (5 \times 7)$$
$$= 32 + 35$$
$$= 67.$$

E Work these out now.

1 $(2 \times 5) + (3 \times 6)$
2 $(4 \times 7) + (5 \times 7)$
3 $(6 \times 6) + (4 \times 4)$
4 $(7 \times 6) - (5 \times 4)$
5 $(8 \times 9) - (9 \times 6)$
6 $(10 \times 7) - (7 \times 8)$
7 $(4 \times 2) \times (3 \times 2)$
8 $(5 \times 2) \times (4 \times 2)$
9 $(24 \div 4) + (30 \div 6)$
10 $(48 \div 6) - (10 \div 2)$
11 $(6 \times 9) \div (3 \times 2)$
12 $(8 \times 5) \div (5 \times 2)$
13 $(9 \times 8) \div (3 \times 8)$
14 $(6 \times 7) \div (4 \times 2)$

Easy problems to make sure

Think well! In some you add, in some you subtract, in some you multiply and in others you divide.

A 1 John has 18 marbles, Tom 15 and Jim 23. How many altogether?

2 Jean had 25 beads. She gave away 14. How many had she left?

3 24 toys were put in boxes. 6 in each box. How many boxes were there?

4 A pencil box holds 10 pencils. How many boxes are needed for 120 pencils?

5 6 boys. Each has 20 marbles. How many altogether?

6 8 boxes. 6 cakes in each box. How many cakes altogether?

7 Jean has 17 beads. How many more to make 30?

8 180 boys are standing in rows. 9 boys in each row. How many rows?

9 What must be added to 38 to make 100?

10 There are 185 pages in Donald's book. He has read 69 of them. How many pages has he still to read?

B 1 There are 11 players in a football team. How many teams can be made up from 44 boys?

2 210 children go on an outing to the zoo. 7 buses take them. How many children in each bus?

3 John is 14 years old. His father is 4 times as old. How old is John's father?

4 Mary had 58 pence in her money box. She spent 23. How many were left?

5 30 children sat down to dinner. 6 children at each table. How many tables?

6 A girl had 84 sweets. She ate 6 each day. How many days did the sweets last?

7 420 children are in 10 classes. If there is the same number in each class, how many are in each class?

8 96 eggs in one box. 48 in another box. How many eggs altogether?

C **1** Sam has 38 marbles. How many short of 100?

2 18 boys in each row. How many in 5 rows?

3 3 dozen eggs in a box. 4 were broken. How many not broken?

4 400 cakes are in 10 boxes. If the same number is in each box, how many cakes in a box?

5 Tom has 20 marbles. Jim has 8 more than Tom and Jack has 7 more than Jim. How many has Jack?

6 23 rows of soldiers. 8 in each row. How many soldiers?

7 90 boys. 6 in each row. How many rows?

8 72 bars of chocolate are in 6 boxes. If the same number is in each box, how many bars in a box?

D **1** Jim and Fred have 170 marbles between them. Jim has 52. How many has Fred?

2 I had 72 pennies in my money box. I spent a quarter of them. How many had I left?

3 1 day has 24 hours. How many hours in 5 days?

4 280 seats. 10 in each row. How many rows?

5 I have 420 stamps to put in a book of 6 pages. How many should I put on each page?

6 A box holds 30 bottles of milk. How many bottles in 8 full boxes?

7 Father gives Jim a fifty. Mother gives him 2 tens. He spends 45p. How much money has he left?

8 9 rows of chairs. 24 in each row. How many chairs altogether?

E **1** John is 15 years old. His grandfather is 5 times as old. How old is his grandfather?

2 There were 48 people in a bus. At the first stop, 9 got off and 14 came on. How many are in the bus now?

3 64 girls were arranged in 4 equal rows. How many were in each row?

4 Father gave Sue 3 tens and 1 five. Mother gave her 2 tens and 1 two. She spent 25p. How much money had she left?

5 A sheet of stamps has 24 in a row, and there are 6 rows. How many stamps are in the sheet?

6 If John has 19 marbles and Fred has 34, how many more has Fred than John?

7 John brought 16 cakes to my party. Mary brought 12, Jean brought 19. How many cakes were brought?

8 How many skipping-ropes, 2 metres long, can be cut from a rope 30 metres long?

Square numbers

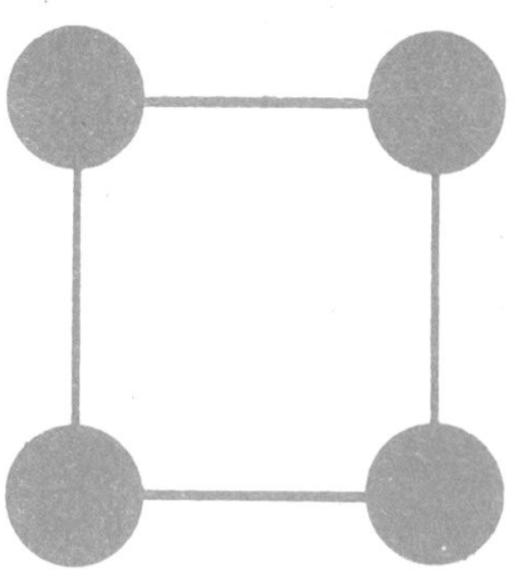

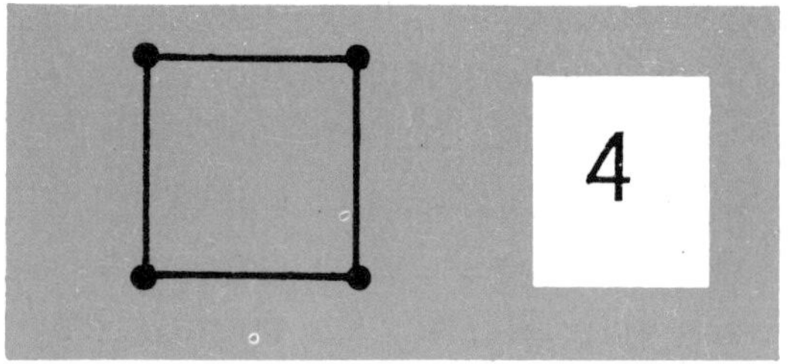

Look at this pattern. You can see there are 2 rows of dots and 2 columns of dots. These make a 2×2 square.
$2 \times 2 = 4$, so 4 is called a **Square Number**.

Here is another pattern.
We have 3 rows of dots and 3 columns of dots.
$3 \times 3 = 9$
9 is a **Square Number**.

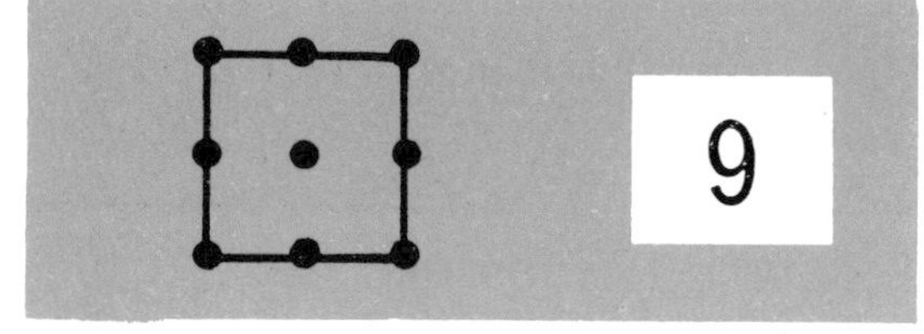

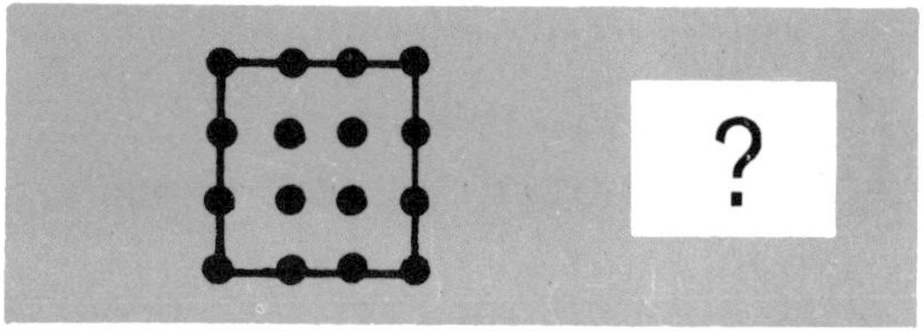

Look at this pattern.
How many dots are there?
Is this a Square Number? Why?

Here is a short way of writing Square Numbers.

$4 = 2 \times 2 = 2^2$ (We call this "Two Squared").
$9 = 3 \times 3 = 3^2$ (We call this "Three Squared").
$16 = 4 \times 4 = 4^2$ (What do we call this?)

Make up the patterns of dots for the next three square numbers. You could use a peg-board for making your patterns if you like.

at numbers do these stand for ?

5^2	7^2	9^2
6^2	8^2	10^2

B Which of these are Square Numbers ?

12	18	36	64
16	25	60	50

C Work these out. The first one is done for you.

1 $6^2 - 3^2 = (6 \times 6) - (3 \times 3) = 36 - 9 = 27$

2 $3^2 + 2^2 =$ 4 $4^2 + 3^2 =$ 6 $4^2 - 1^2 =$ 8 $6^2 + 4^2 =$

3 $5^2 - 3^2 =$ 5 $5^2 - 4^2 =$ 7 $4^2 + 2^2 =$ 9 $10^2 - 5^2 =$

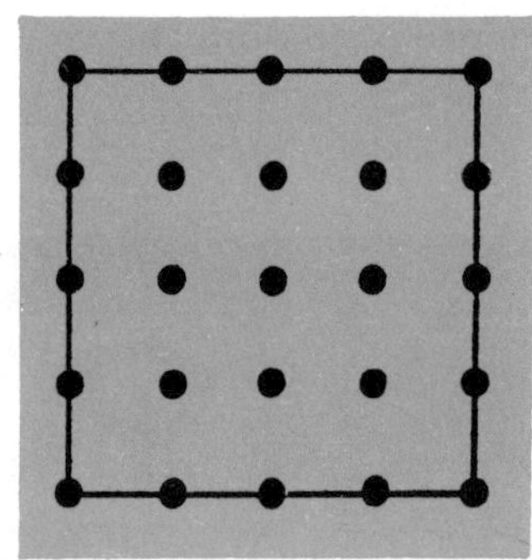

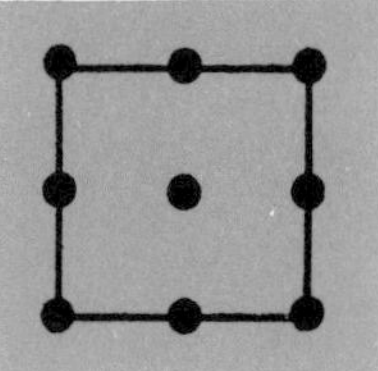

Show your answer in a pattern. Try to make up some of your own.

D You can use the squares in your exercise book to show square numbers.

(a) 1

(b)

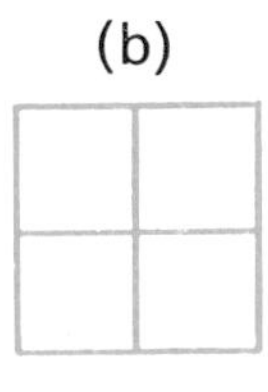

$2 \times 2 = 2^2$

(c)

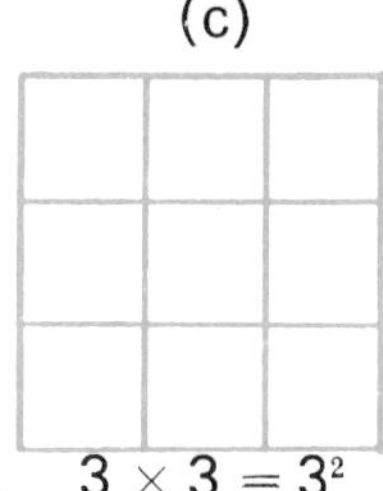

$3 \times 3 = 3^2$

Draw a larger square like this to show that $4 \times 4 = 4^2 = 16$.
Draw another square to show that $5 \times 5 = 5^2 = 25$.

Draw figure (c). Colour in 4 boxes.
How many are left ?
So that $3^2 - 2^2 = 9 - 4 = 5$.

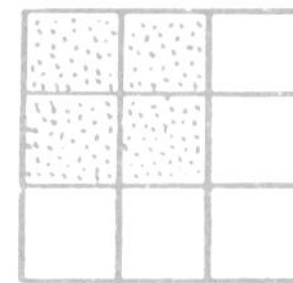

Rectangle numbers

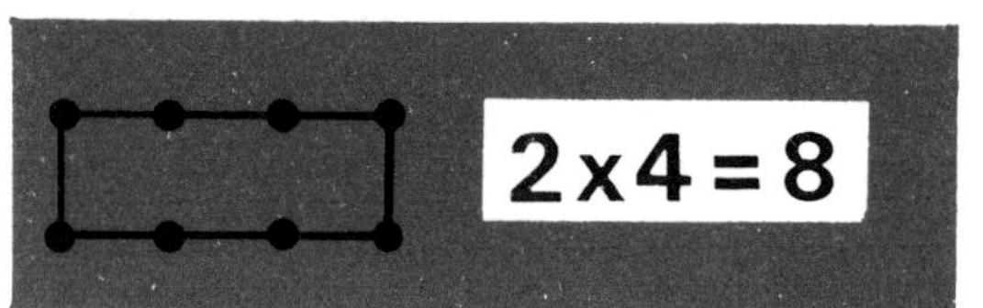

Why do you think 8 is called a rectangle number?

Is this a rectangle number?
Which number is it?
Make this pattern on your peg board and then copy it into your exercise book.

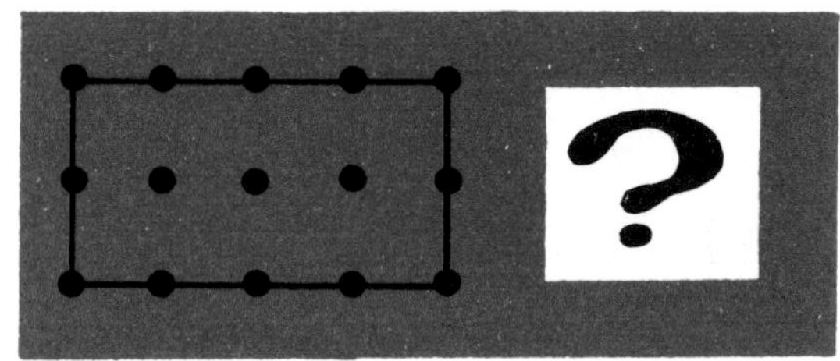

Find some more rectangle numbers by making patterns on your peg board and in your exercise book. Under each pattern write the number.

Without making patterns can you say which of the following numbers are rectangle numbers and which are square numbers?

6 9 12 18 24 25 30 36

Let's try to arrange 5 in the shape of rectangle. You will see we can't do it.

Try to make rectangles with
3, 7, 11, 13.
Numbers like these which you can't make into squares or rectangles are called *prime* numbers.

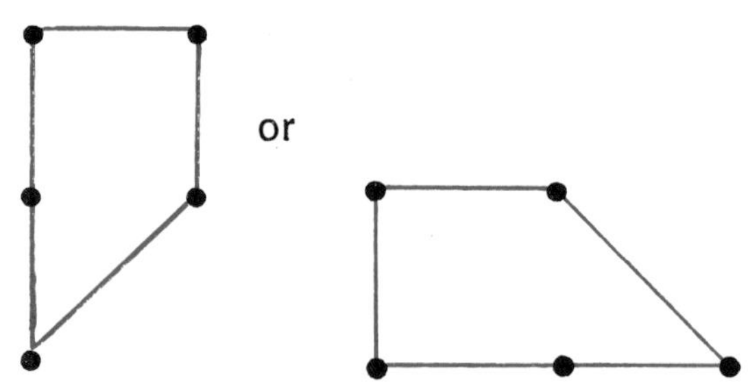

Triangles

(A)

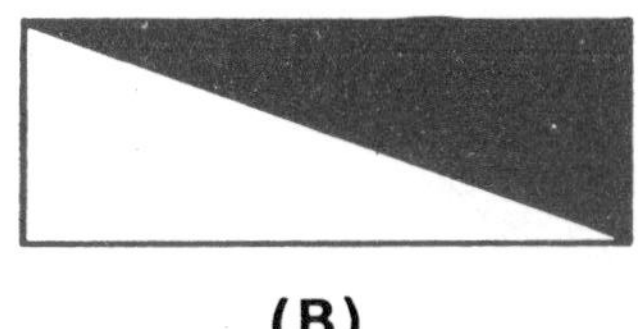

(B)

When we were "drawing" pictures with different shapes, we divided squares and rectangles into two by joining opposite corners.

If you cut along this "dividing" line, you would get two triangles from each. How many sides has a triangle? How many corners (or angles) has a triangle?
These triangles would have one of their corners (or angles) a right angle. You can test this with your right angle measure.

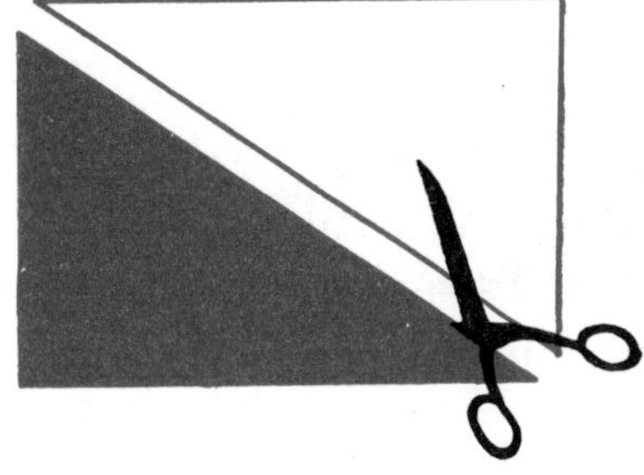

Measure the sides of the coloured triangle in shape (A).
What do you find?
Measure the sides of the coloured triangle in shape (B).
What do you find?
In (A) the triangle has two equal sides.
In (B) the triangle has none of its sides equal.

A Measure the sides of these triangles, and write down how many sides are equal.

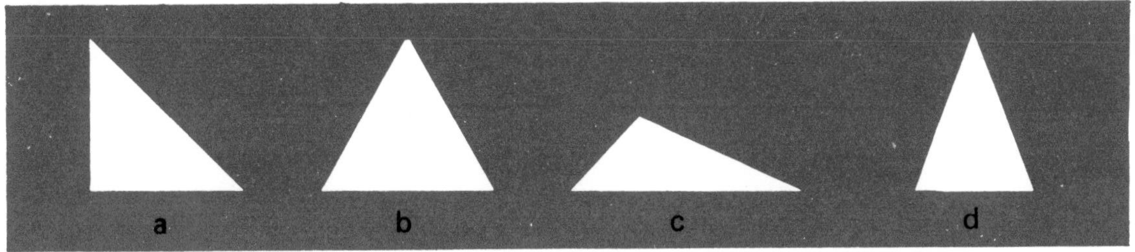

Some triangles have 3 sides equal
Some triangles have 2 sides equal
Some triangles have No sides equal

B Get 3 milk straws, or pencils, or rulers of the same length. Find 2 more of different lengths.
Now use them to make triangles like this :—

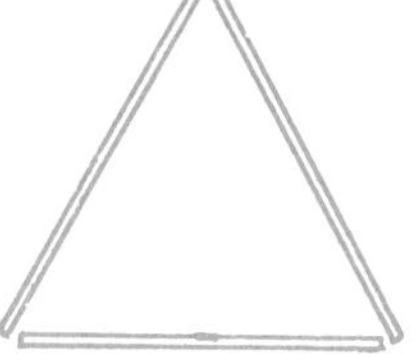

3 sides equal

2 sides equal

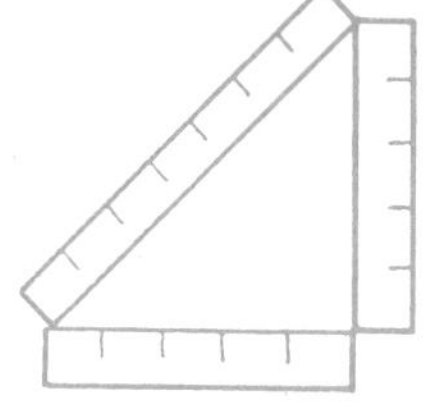
2 sides equal
(and a right angle)

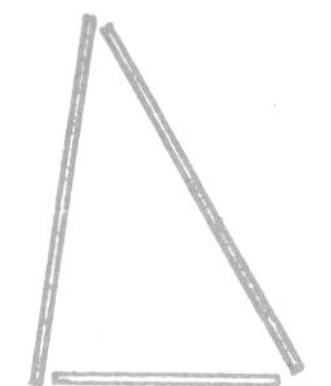
No sides equal

C Make some triangles on your nail-board with rubber bands.
Could you make a triangle on your board which has its three sides equal ? Try it.

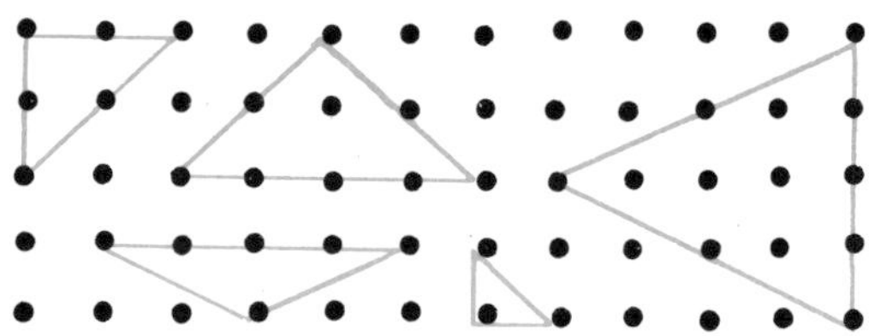

D

You can even make triangle shapes by putting three books, or exercise books together.
Will this triangle have one of its corners or angles a right angle ?

Try to make one with three match-boxes. What can you say about this triangle ?

E Look around you outside and see if you can find some things in the shape of triangles. Make a list, or draw them. Say whether all the sides are equal, or only two of them, or none. Say which have a right angle corner. Here are some to help you.

Envelope Flap

Chocolate Biscuit

Traffic Sign

Cub Scarf

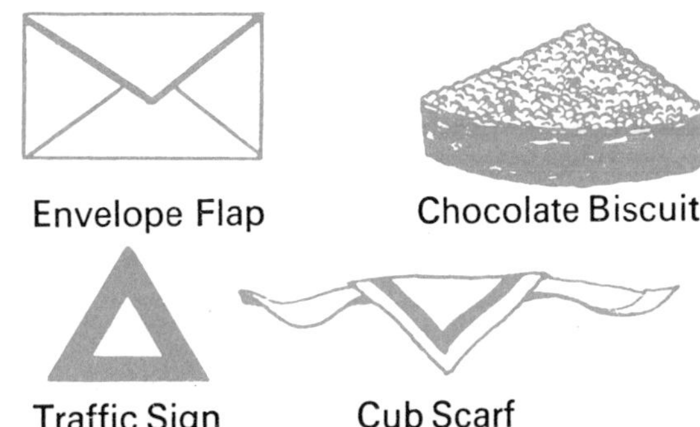

F Cut out different kinds of triangles and make some patterns with them, like these.

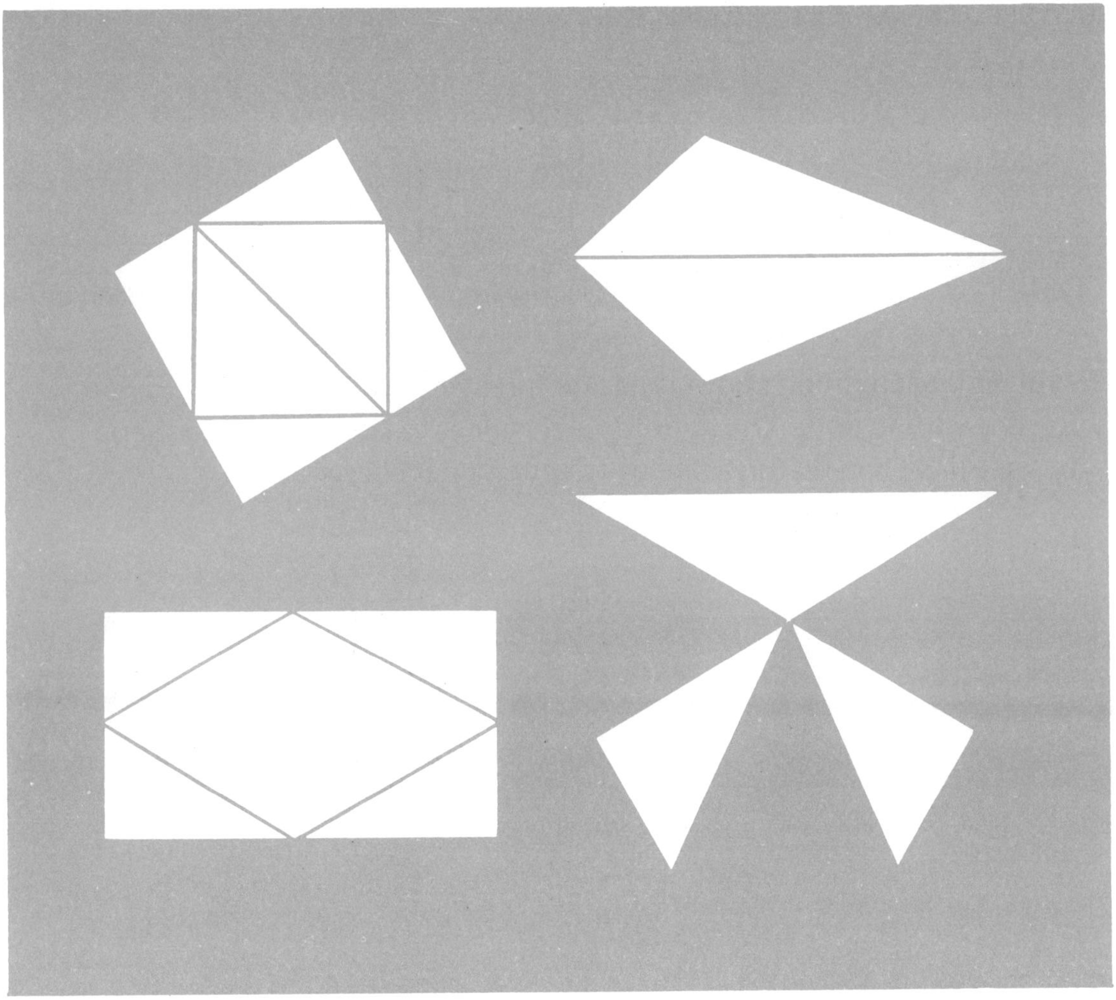

Symmetry

Here are some interesting pictures.

			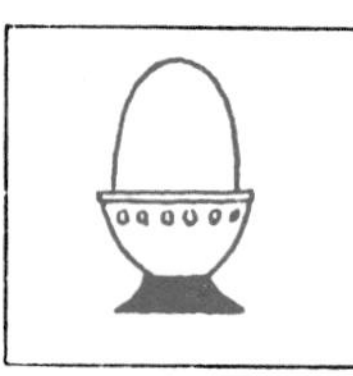	
Bell	Vase	Pillar Box	Egg Cup	Parachute

Do you notice anything about these pictures?
If you draw a line down the middle, each side is exactly the same shape.
Let us see if we can do the same by folding paper shapes.

A Take a square of coloured paper.

		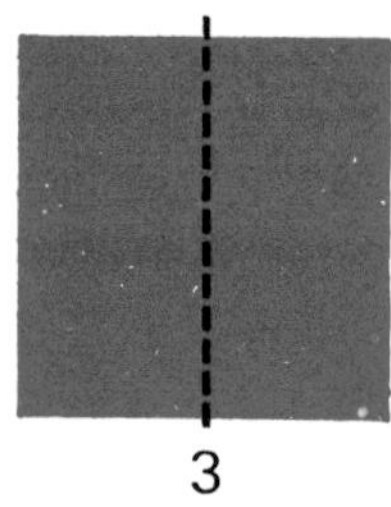	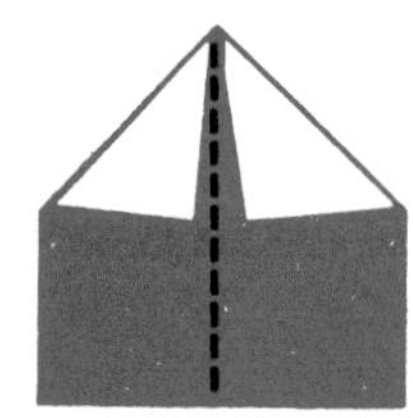	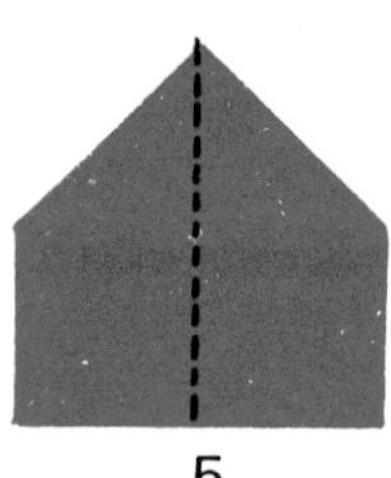
1 Coloured Square	2 Fold down the middle	3 Open out	4 Fold in top corners (or cut off)	5 What does this look like?

If you fold shape 5 about the dotted line, you will see that the right half fits exactly over the left half.

B Take a circle of folded paper.

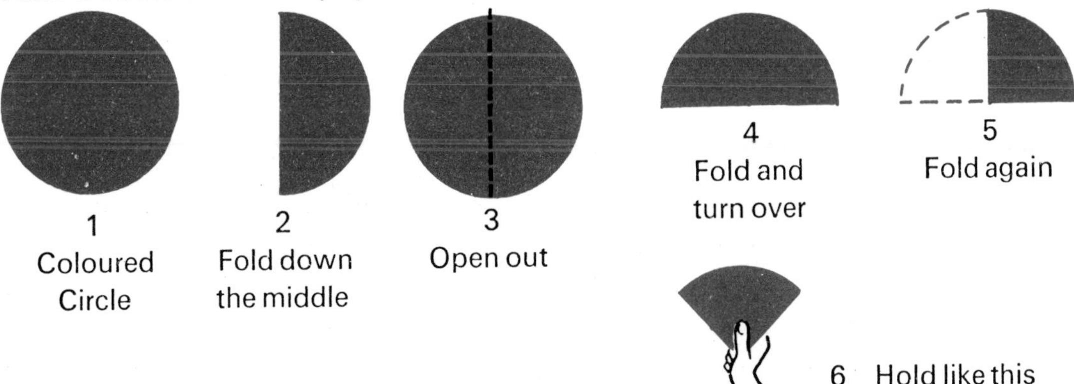

1 Coloured Circle — 2 Fold down the middle — 3 Open out — 4 Fold and turn over — 5 Fold again — 6 Hold like this

Shape 1 is a . . . . . .
Shape 2 is like a half- . . . . . .
Shape 4 is like a tea- . . . . . .
Shape 6 is like a . . . . . .

Did you find, as you folded each time that the shapes fitted exactly about the fold ?
Test by unfolding and folding back again.

C Take another coloured square.

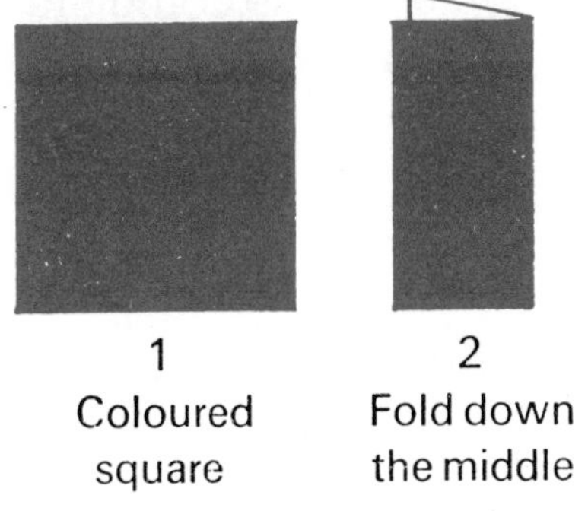

1 Coloured square — 2 Fold down the middle

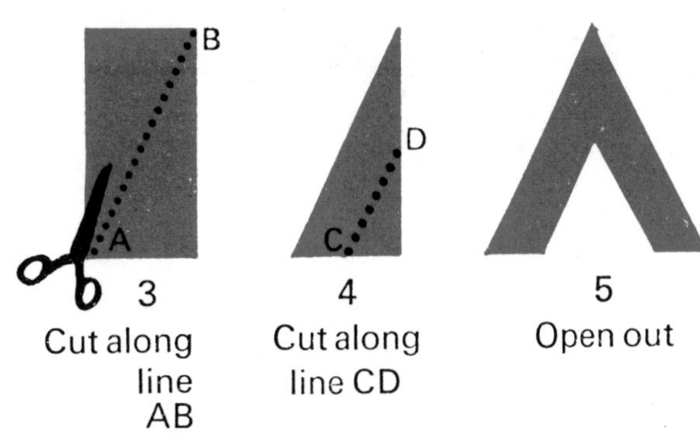

3 Cut along line AB — 4 Cut along line CD — 5 Open out

Shape 1 is a S - - - - e.
Shape 2 is a R - - - - - - - e.
Shape 4 is a T - - - - - - e.

Shape 5 is like a W - - - - m.
(Think of Red Indians !)

You can put together the two pieces left from shape (3) to form a triangle. If you open out the small bit left from Shape (4) you will have another triangle. Notice again how each half fits over the other when you fold.

D Try to make these shapes on a nail-board. Use a long elastic band for the "fold". One side of the shape has been put in. Can you make the other side of the shape with elastic bands. ?

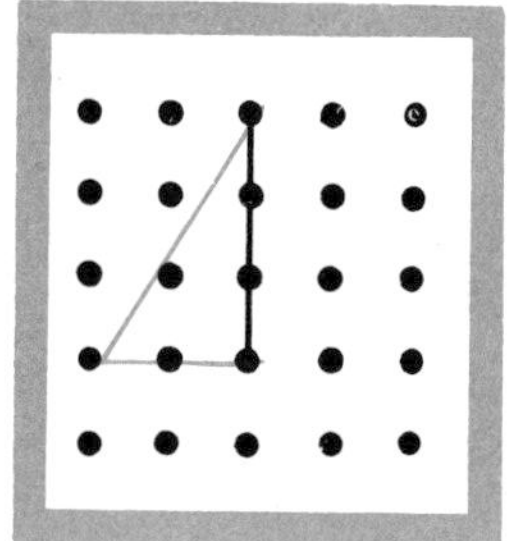 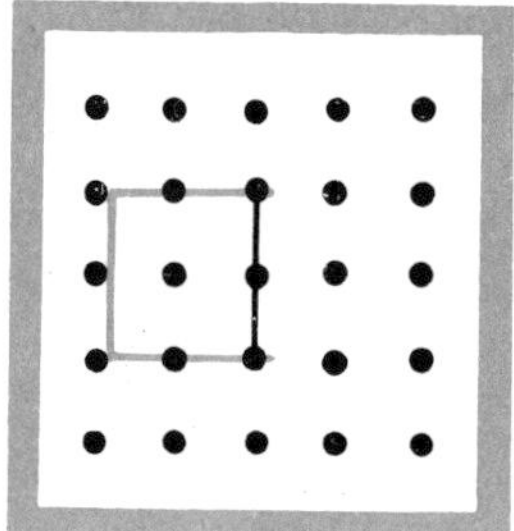 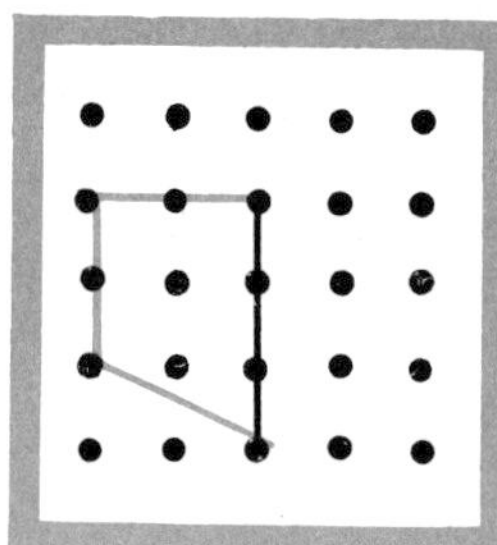 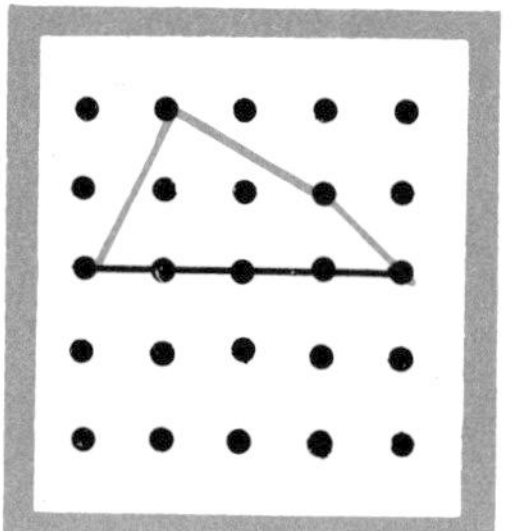

Now make some shapes of your own on the board. Make sure the "fold" divides your shape into two equal parts. The "fold" is called a "Line of Symmetry".

Did you notice that if you traced these shapes on paper and folded them about the "black" line, they would fit over one another exactly ?

E Here are some "half-shapes". Now put a thin, flat mirror on the "fold". If you look at the mirror and the "half-shape", you should see the complete shape. The "half-shape", and the "mirror shape" are the same, but the other way round.

In this half-shape we see half of a boy's face. But in the "mirror shape" the right ear is on the left, and so on.

Using a thin flat mirror on the fold, what are these ?

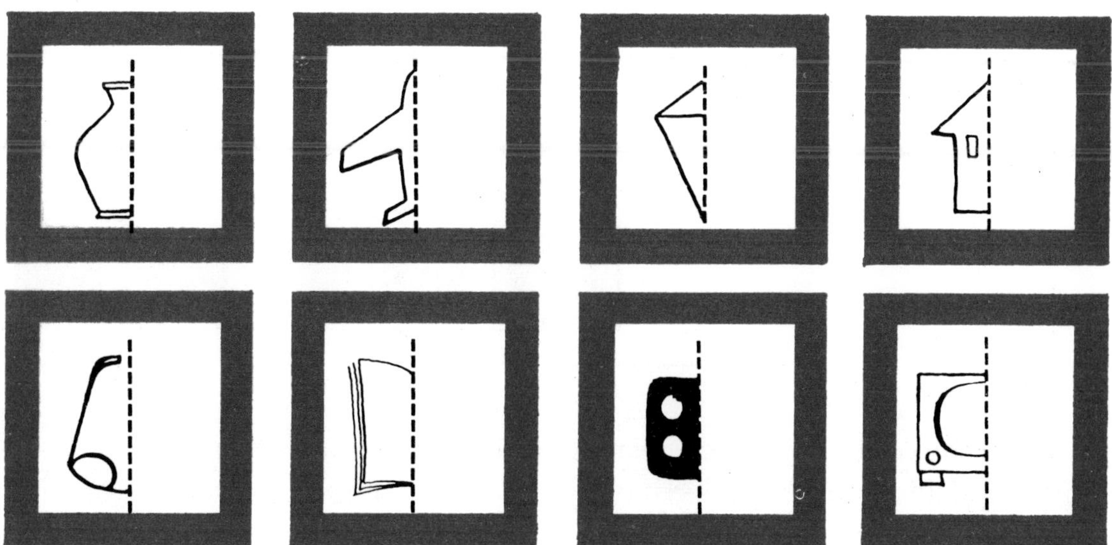

Try to draw the "mirror picture" which appears on the other side of the "fold", or mirror edge.

Tiles and patterns

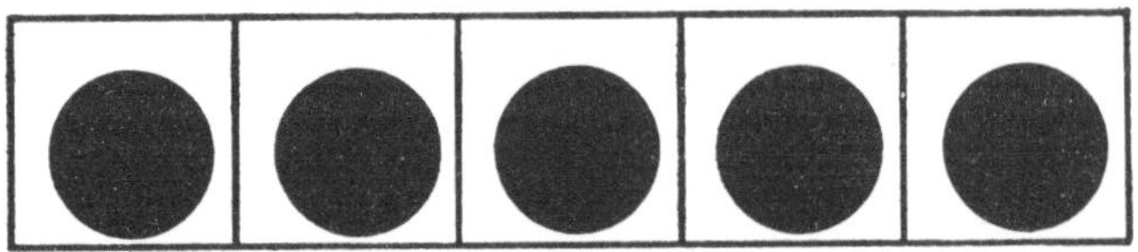

A Some of the walls in your school may be tiled. Floors are often tiled with squares of linoleum or blocks of wood. Here are some tile patterns. Copy them, and continue the pattern. The left side shows you how the patterns are made. Use squared paper, and colour in the patterns.

Strips or Borders

This is made from tiles which are rectangles.

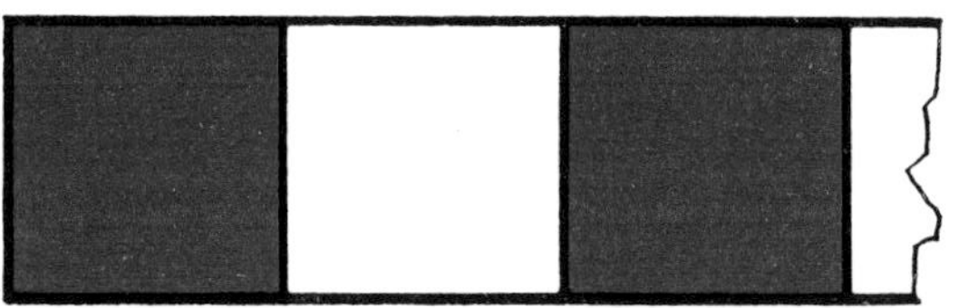

This is made from tiles which are squares.

Here we divide the rectangles into triangles.

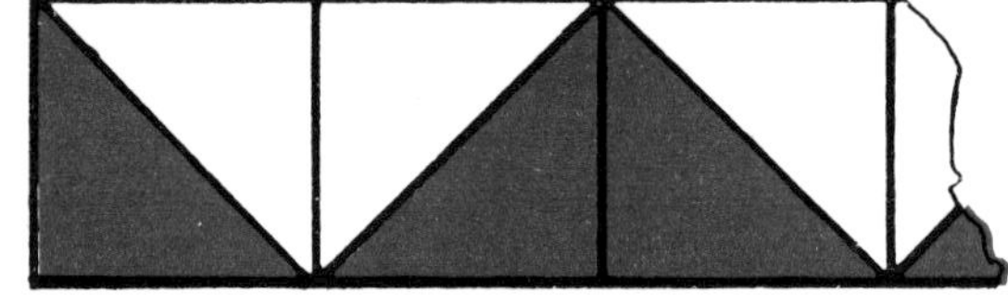

Here we divide each square into two triangles.

Here we have squares and some of the squares are divided into 2 triangles.

Now make up some borders of your own, using squares and rectangles, and also squares and rectangles divided into triangles.

B Checks and Chess boards

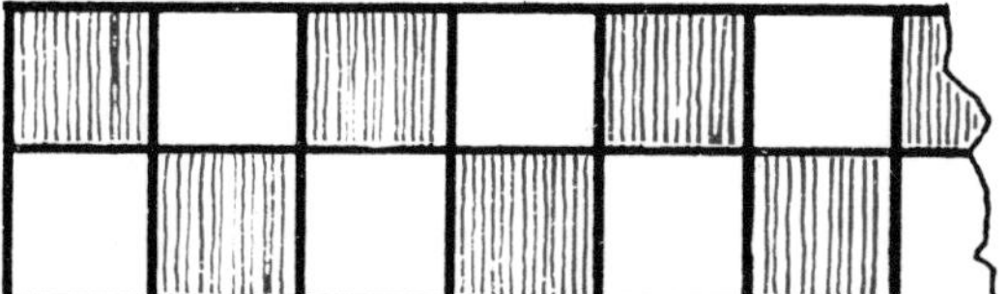

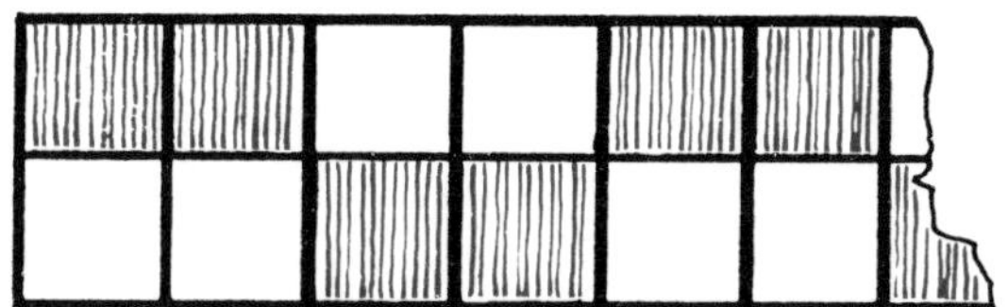

Continue these patterns to left and right, and also above and below. Have you seen a chess-board, or a draught board ? Count the squares and try to draw one in colour in your exercise-book .

C Draw these patterns in your book and continue them across your page.

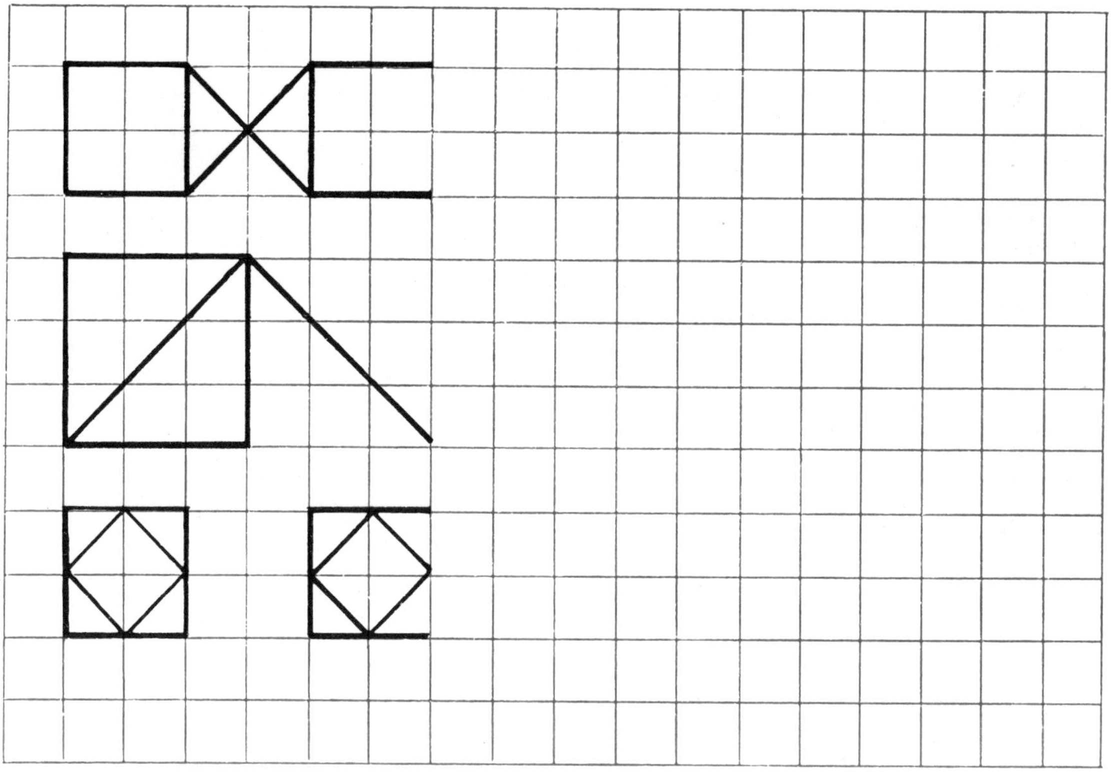

Solids

A

When a pond is frozen, you can skate on the surface of the pond. It is a sheet or surface of ice. If you swim in a pond, your body would be below the surface. A surface can be flat or it can be curved.

If you lay your exercise book flat on your desk,the outside cover is a flat surface.

If you pick up your exercise book and curl it, the surface will be curved.

Which of these have flat surfaces and which have curved surfaces ?

1 the black-board.
2 a football.
3 the top of a table.
4 the side of a tin of soup.
5 a window pane.
6 an electric bulb.
7 the top of your head.
8 the walls of a room.

A flat surface can be horizontal, as the top of a table, or it can be vertical, like a wall in your classroom, or it may be slanting (or oblique) like the side of a tent.

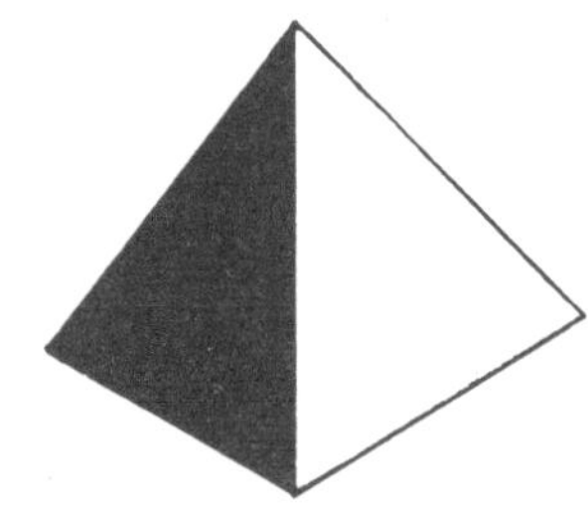

B Here is a cube.

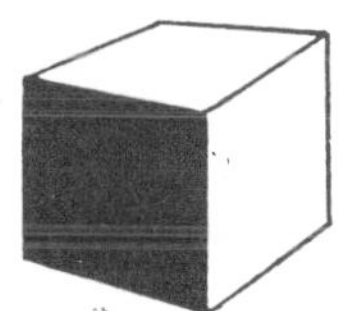

You have seen Oxo cubes or sugar cubes. Many boxes are in the shape of a cube and you may have some cubes in your school. The faces of a cube are flat surfaces. How many flat surfaces or faces has the cube?

1 If we put the cube on a flat table, how many horizontal faces has it, and how many vertical faces?

2 What is the shape of each face of a cube?

3 How many edges has the cube? Count them. Edges are lines.

4 Point out two surfaces which meet. What separates these two surfaces? Here is a tent with two oblique surfaces. In each case a line separates the two surfaces.

C 5 If you have a cube, chalk the line separating the two surfaces.

Here is a solid like a cube. We call it a cuboid. Cuboid means "like a cube".

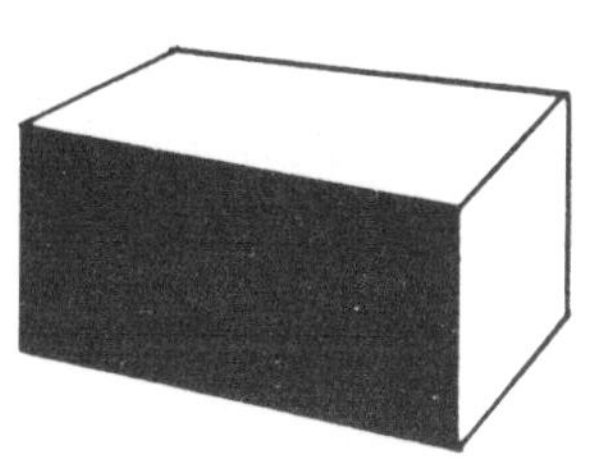

Are the faces of a cuboid flat or curved? The faces of a cube are all the same size and have all the same shape. Is this true of the cuboid? What can you say about the faces of the cuboid? Can you now say how a cuboid differs from a cube?

See how many things you can collect which are cubes or cuboids— Oxo cube, Corn Flake Packet, and so on.

Take a pile of 2p coins and arrange them neatly one on top of another and you will get this shape.

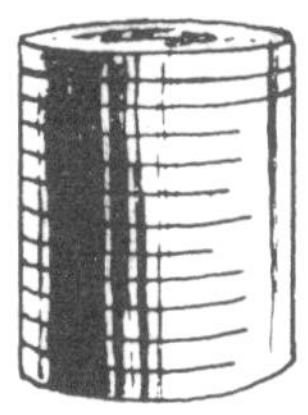

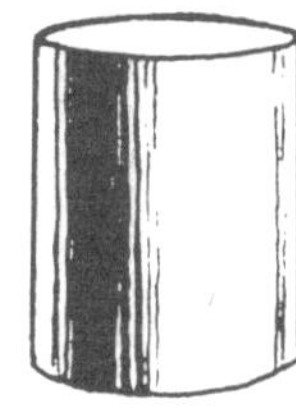

or laid flat

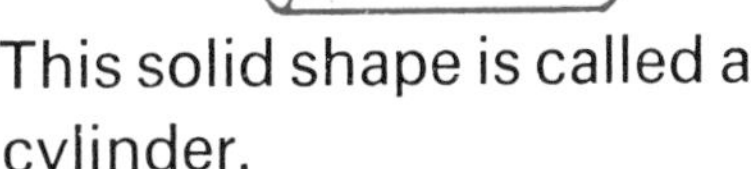

This solid shape is called a cylinder.

What things have you seen which are cylinders?
See how many cylinder shaped objects you can collect. We could make a cylinder, too, by taking round counters or discs, all exactly the same size, and putting them neatly on top of another. Try this.

E If we cut out a lot of triangles, all exactly the same size, we could make a solid like this. or laid flat

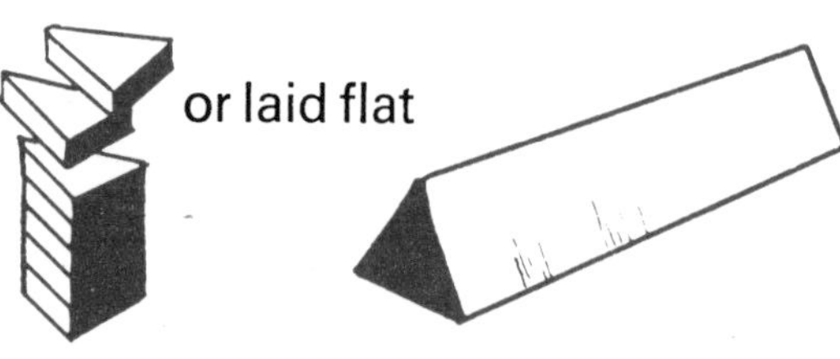

Where have you seen this shape? Could you bring one to school?

Shapes which can be made like this by piling shapes all exactly the same size, on top of each other neatly, are called **Prisms.** The prism above (laid flat) is called a **triangular** prism. Think hard and say why it gets this name. Why triangular?

F

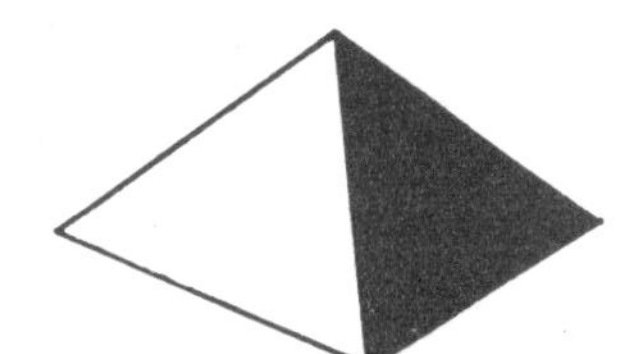

Look at this solid. Could we pile up shapes all exactly the same to make it? Would it be right to call it a prism? Why not?
This is called a **Pyramid**. Can you now say how a pyramid differs from a prism? Think hard.

G Here is a shape you should know. Do you know what it is called? (Here's a hint. You often buy ice-cream in a shape like this, though then it is always the other way round.)
What shapes, taking smaller and smaller sizes each time until you reach the top, could you use to make a solid shape like this?

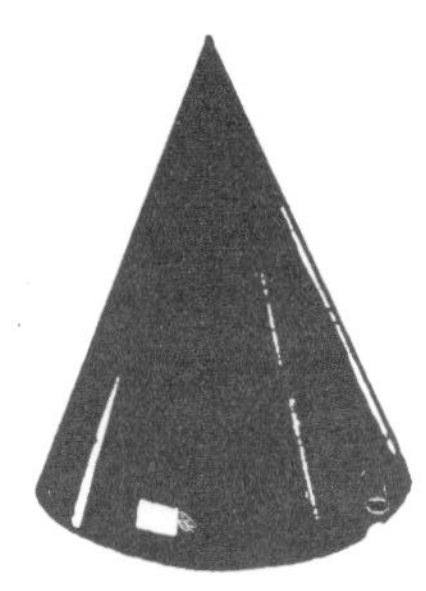

H

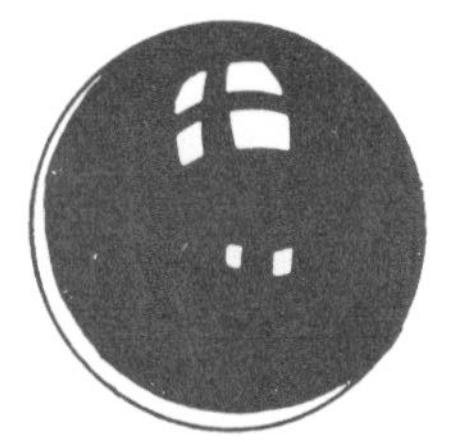

This is a solid which you all know—the shape of a plastic football. Its proper name is a sphere. Things which have the shape of a sphere (ball shaped) are said to be **spherical.**
Name some things which are spherical.

Sets

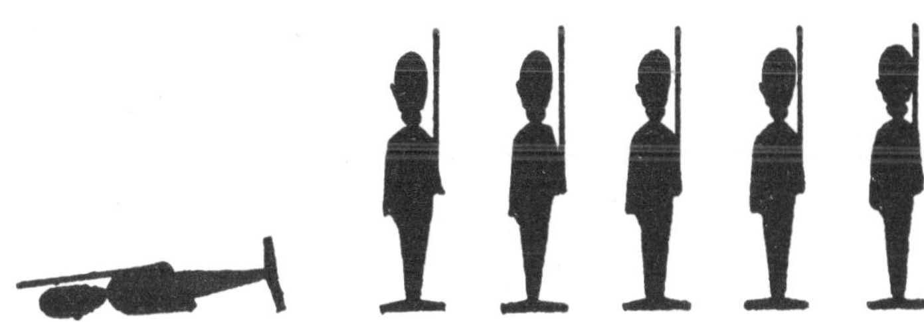

Things are often arranged in sets. In your classroom you have sets of books, sets of pencils, sets of rulers and many other sets. Can you name some other sets you have in your room?

At home your mother has a set of dishes, a set of knives, a set of spoons, a set of pots and pans. Can you name some other sets of things you have at home?

People can also form sets. You could have a set of girls in your class with fair hair, a set of boys with blue eyes, a set of men who play football, a set of ladies who play tennis, and so on.

Can you name some other sets of people?

You see we can have sets of anything.

A Look at these sets. One thing is out of place. It does not belong to the set. Pick it out.

1

3

2

4

Here are some more sets. To keep the things that form a set together we put then inside curly brackets, like these { }

B There is a mistake in each set. One thing does not belong to the set and should not be there. Pick it out.

1 {apple, orange, coal, banana} is a set of fruit.
2 {John, Jim, Bill, Mary} is a set of boys.
3 {cup, book, plate, saucer} is a set of dishes.
4 {ship, cow, horse, sheep} is a set of animals.
5 {boy, girl, man, train} is a set of people.
6 {dress, coat, hen, shirt} is a set of clothing.
7 {eagle, seagull, robin, rabbit} is a set of birds.
8 {red, toy, blue, green} is a set of colours.

C Here are six more sets. One thing is out of place in each set. Pick it out and put it in its right set. If you are writing the sets in your exercise book, don't forget the curly brackets and don't forget to put a comma after each thing in the set. Be sure to say what each set is.

1 {cat, dog, bed, monkey } is a set of animals.
2 {rose, tulip, saucer, daisy} is a set of flowers.
3 {daffodil, chair, table, sofa} is a set of furniture.
4 {apple, plum, robin, pear} is a set of fruit.
5 {sparrow, budgie, canary, horse} is a set of birds.
6 {cup, orange, plate, bowl} is a set of dishes.
7 {cabbage, carrot, dog, turnip} is a set of vegetables.

D Numbers can also form sets. In each of the following sets pick out the number which does not belong to the set.

1 {1, 2, 3, 4, 9, 6} is the set of the first six numbers.
2 {10, 20, 30, 35, 50} is the set of the first five tens.
3 {1, 3, 5, 7, 8, 9} is the set of the odd numbers up to 9.
4 {2, 4, 6, 7, 8, 10} is the set of even numbers up to 10.
5 {100, 200, 300, 350, 400} is the set of the first five hundreds.
6 {600, 700, 750, 800, 900} is the set of the second five hundreds.

Work Cards

1

This picture shows the number of pets the children in a class keep at home.
Each 0 stands for 1 pet.

Dogs	0 0 0 0 0 0 0 0
Cats	0 0 0 0 0 0 0 0 0 0 0 0 0 0 0 0
Rabbits	0 0 0 0 0
Canaries	0 0 0 0 0 0 0 0 0 0 0 0 0 0 0 0 0
Budgies	0 0 0 0 0 0 0 0 0 0 0 0 0 0 0 0 0 0 0 0

1 Write down the number of each pet.
2 How many more cats are there than dogs?
3 How many more budgies than canaries?
4 Find out how many pets are kept by the children in your class, and draw a picture like this one.
4 Instead of pets write down the names of the months of the year. Find out how many children were born in each month and draw a picture like this one.

2

1 If n = 36 ÷ 4, find the number n stands for?
2 y = 8 × 5. Find what y is.
3 a = (6 × 4) + 10. Find the value of a.
4 (7 × 3) + (9 × 2) = b. What number does b stand for?
5 y = (8 × 4) + (6 × 5). Find what y is.

6 Count the letters in this word:
WOLVERHAMPTON
How many letters are there?
If you wrote the word three times how many letters would you have?
7 How many gloves are there in a dozen pairs?
8 What are the next three numbers?
5 10 15 20 ? ? ?

3 Fill a litre measure with water.
Find how many school milk bottles can be filled from 1 litre.
Use a funnel to pour the water into the bottles.
Now make up a table like this and put in the numbers.
How many bottles of milk were drunk in your class this morning?
About how many litres was this?

Litres	Number of bottles
1	
2	
3	
4	
5	
6	

4

Find the missing numbers.

1. $7 \times 6 = ?$
2. $36 \div 3 = ?$
3. $32 - 12 = ?$
4. $8 \times 9 = ?$
5. $(6 \times 7) - 2 = ?$
6. $72 \div 9 = ?$

5

Find the missing numbers.

1. $7 + ? = 15$
2. $8 \times ? = 56$
3. $(9 \times 8) - ? = 69$
4. $42 \div ? = 7$
5. $(\frac{1}{2} \text{ of } 4) + (\frac{1}{3} \text{ of } 9) = ?$
6. $(\frac{1}{3} \text{ of } 12) - (\frac{1}{4} \text{ of } 8) = ?$

6 This picture shows how many of each coin 5 boys have saved up in their money boxes.

	10p	5p	2p	1p	½p
Tom	1	2	5	8	4
Ken	4	6	3	8	2
Jim	3	5	6	12	6
Dan	2	4	4	10	8
Joe	-	8	2	5	-

(a) How much money has each boy saved?
(b) Who saved most?
(c) How much more has Ken saved than Dan?
(d) How much less than 50p have Tom and Joe saved?
(e) How much less than 100p has each boy saved?

7

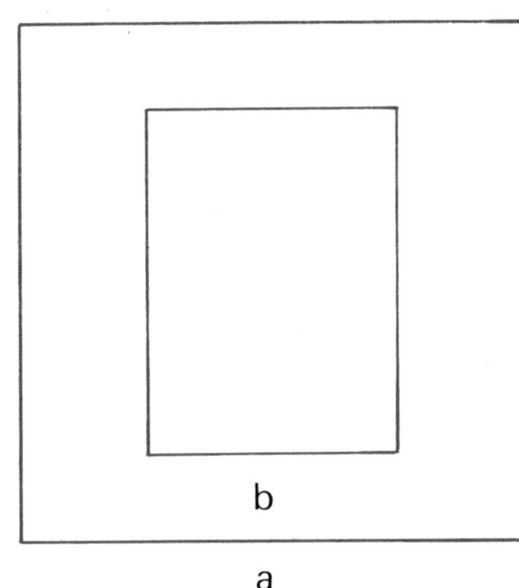

1 Measure the length of each side of shape a.
Find the length all round shape a.
What kind of shape is shape a?

2 Measure the length of each side of shape b.
Find the length all round shape b.
What kind of shape is shape b?

8

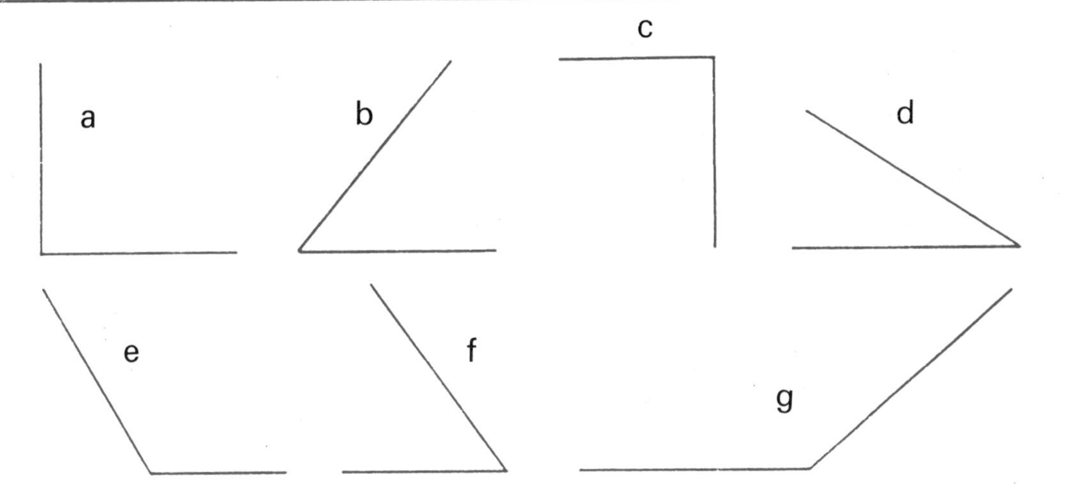

1 Use your right angle to test these angles.
(**a**) Which of the angles are right angles?
(**b**) Which of them are smaller than a right angle?
(**c**) Which are bigger than a right angle?

2 It is a good idea to have a Book of Shapes. In it draw
(**a**) two right angles.
(**b**) two angles smaller than a right angle.
(**c**) two angles bigger than a right angle.

9

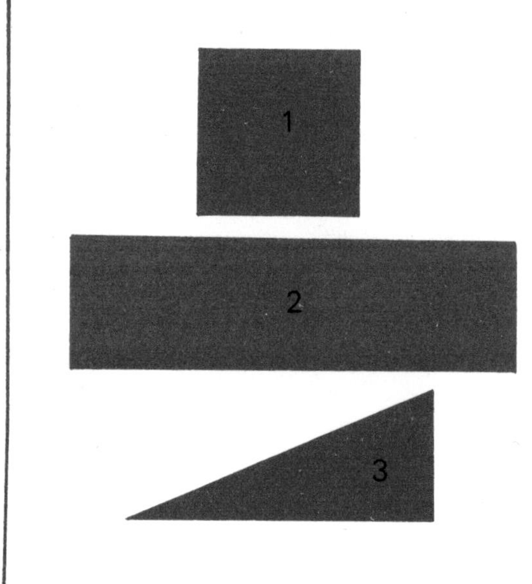

1 a What do you call this shape?
b How many square corners (right angles) has it?
c What do you know about its sides?
2 a What is this shape called?
b How many right angles has it?
c In what way is it different from a square?
3 a What is this shape called?
b How many right angles has it?
c Could you draw a triangle with two right angles?
4 Draw these shapes in your Book of Shapes and write the name of each shape below it.

10

Poland
Holland
Czechoslovakia
France
Belgium
Finland

Here are the flags of six countries. Draw them in your squared-paper book. Find out the colours on the flags and colour your flags in the same way.
1 What is the shape of each flag?
2 Which flag has two different coloured rectangles?
3 Which flags have three different coloured rectangles?
4 Which flag has a cross?
5 What colour is this cross?
6 Which flag has a triangle in it?
7 What shape is each of the other two parts of this flag?
8 Which flag has two small squares in it?
Draw some flags of your own and colour them.

11

1 In the playground draw a line with chalk. From this measure 30 cm and put a mark there. Then mark off another 30 cm and so on for about 240 cm.
Now see who can jump 30 cm, 75 cm, 100 cm and so on.
Count the number in the class who can jump these lengths and make a box picture to show this.

2 Make another box picture showing the number of children who can jump a height of 30 cm, 60 cm, 90 cm.

3 Make a list of some children's programmes on T.V. Ask the children in your class which they like best. Count the number for each programme and draw a box picture.

12

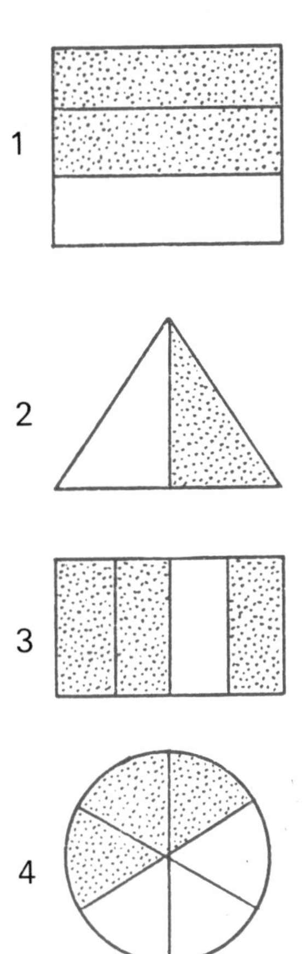

Write down the name of each shape.

1 How many parts is shape 1 divided into?
How many parts of it are coloured?
What fraction (part) of it is coloured?
What fraction (part) of it is not coloured?

2 How many parts is shape 2 divided into?
What fraction (part) of it is coloured?
What fraction of it is not coloured?

3 How many parts is shape 3 divided into?
How many parts are coloured?
What fraction is not coloured?

4 How many parts is shape 4 divided into?
How many parts are coloured?
What fraction of the shape is coloured?
What fraction is not coloured?

5 Draw in your squared paper book a shape like shape 3. Colour two parts. What fraction of the shape is this? What fraction of the shape have you not coloured?

6 Draw round a penny to make shape 4.
Divide it into six equal parts.
Colour four parts. What fraction have you coloured?
What fraction is not coloured?

13

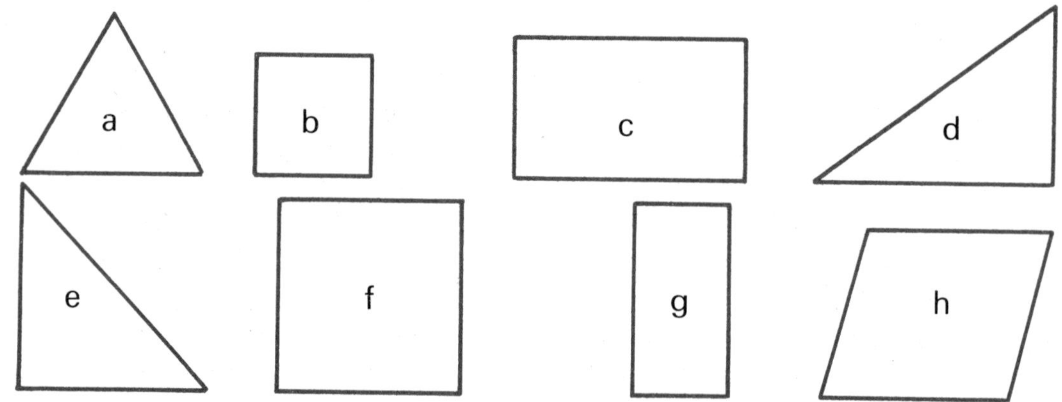

1 Copy these shapes, except shape h, in your squared paper exercise book, but make them much bigger. Under each shape write its name.
2 Which shapes have one right angle?
3 Which shapes have 4 right angles?
4 Is shape h a square? Why not?

14 Copy the table and show the number of coins needed to make up each amount of money.
The first one is done for you.

Amounts	50p	10p	5p	2p	1p
27p		2	1	1	
26p					
18p					
57p					
74p					
38p					
83p					
79p					

M Kirkpatrick